EXPLORING STA

AND

SURROUNDING VILLAGES

A tour of Stamford and the villages within a six mile
radius of the town.

by

Ian Bishop

Ian Bishop.

Jema Publications

Published 1998 by Jema Publications

© Ian Bishop

ISBN 1 871468 78 7

Publisher's Note
Every care has been taken in the preparation of this book and all
the information has been carefully checked and is believed to be
correct at the time of publication. However, neither the author nor
the publisher can except responsibility for any errors or omissions
or for any loss, damage, injury or inconvenience resulting from
the use of this book.

All maps are based upon the Ordnance Survey Maps and used
with permission of The Controller of Her Majesty's Stationery
Office, © Crown copyright.

Jema Publications
40 Ashley Lane
Moulton
Northampton
NN3 7TJ

Printed in Great Britain by Intype, Wimbledon, London.

CONTENTS

INTRODUCTION

This guide is the second in a continuing series of Exploring....Villages titles; the first, centred around Oundle in Northamptonshire, was published in 1995. As before, I have again started out with a basic 10 kilometre (six mile) circle around the main town; this time Stamford, but have stretched the outer limits occasionally to incorporate places of interest nearby.

There has been no intention to supply the full history of a town or village. Rather the aim has been to provide some information on what travellers, be they on foot, bicycle, in a car or on horseback, may see on their journey although historical notes are included where appropriate. Hopefully the knowledge thus gained may also encourage visitors to seek out places to which they may not otherwise have gone.

However, even a 10km or 6 mile radius circle is over 300 square kilometres (100 square miles) and there will be some gaps and omissions. If there are glaring errors please write to me care of the publisher; should a second edition follow I will endeavour to make relevant corrections. The area has been split into three roughly equal segments, plus the town of Stamford separately. The first covers the villages to the south and west of the A1; the second, those to the east of the A1 and south of the A16; the third, those to the east of the A1 and north of the A16. There are also appendices covering topics of general interest.

It has been a lot of fun gleaning information from visits to each village and also from books, leaflets, village and church guides and maps. It has also been very instructive talking to people about their villages or places of interest and my wife and I have had many a wholesome meal in convivial country pubs.

Considerable use has been made of the Ordnance Survey 1:50,000 Landranger and 1:25,000 Explorer and Pathfinder maps of the area and I would encourage all who read this book to get copies for themselves as they are an invaluable aid for planning routes and getting a feeling for the landscape. Details are in the Bibliography and other published sources are also listed there. Most are still in print and well worth purchasing from your local Bookseller.

My special thanks go to all those people who have helped along the way with directions, anecdotes and assistance. In particular I would like to mention the enthusiastic Alan Blake, former manager of Sacrewell and Val Green, general manager of Tallington Lakes, along with the staff of several inns and public houses.

Ian Bishop
June 1998

Dedicated to my wife, Kathryn, who not only walked many miles with me, visited pubs and helped with research, but also allowed me to get out of some of the housework during the writing of this book.

2

STAMFORD

Ninety miles from London and eighty from Birmingham, if ever a town deserved the motto of another place it is this one. "Multum in Parvo" is the motto of Rutland County (qv) but eminently describes Stamford. In the ellipse of the old walled town, about one kilometre by 400m there are over six hundred buildings of historical interest. With a population of around 18,000, each Friday sees an incredibly busy street market which occupies most of the pedestrianised areas of the old town. There are several pay and display car parks around the town (see map).

Described by Sir Walter Scott as "the finest scene between London and Edinburgh" Stamford has been a strategic place from before the Roman conquest. Indeed at one time it was on the only route from north to south. Now bypassed by the A1 on a monstrous flyover, it is best approached from the south from the roundabout near to Burghley Park. Driving down the road via St Martin's Without the visitor cannot help but notice the gallows sign of the George Inn straddling the road and put up to deter the dishonest from entering the town. The town is on the River Welland and there are five ancient churches and as many chapels. Stated to be "the finest stone town in England", in 1967 it was the first to be declared a conservation area and in 1993 the BBC filmed "Middlemarch" around the town.

The town is mostly built of local limestone known as "Rag", some from nearby Barnack quarries. There was a Roman camp here and Ermine Street passes through the town along Roman Bank and Water Furlong to the ford. There is a monument here to Queen Boudica who pursued the legendary Ninth Legion across the river here. Later it became the assembly point for the army that compelled King John to sign the Magna Carta in 1215.

Recorded in the Domesday Book as a market, development followed in Saxon times and the Danes made it a capital of the Fens. It had a Norman castle and later in the 12th century it became a wool centre, whose cloth was renowned throughout Europe. In Medieval times Stamford was also a place of religious learning. In the wall of the old Grammar School is 14th century Brazenose Gate former entrance to Brazenose Hall. From 1333-

1336 rebellious students from Oxford studied at the Hall and it was the "Brazen Nosed" bull door handle from there which was eventually installed in what is now Brazenose College, Oxford in 1890.

There was much destruction during the Wars of the Roses and during the Civil War Cromwell's forces sacked parts of the town. Eventually the Lordship of the town was granted to 1st Lord Burghley by Elizabeth I. Later still, its wealthy merchants built elegant Georgian, Queen Anne and Tudor houses, designed by the Adams brothers, Inigo Jones and John Thorpe. The Stamford Mercury is the oldest provincial weekly newspaper in the kingdom. Sir Malcolm Sargent, the famous conductor was buried here in 1967.

Before the railways came in the mid 19th century Stamford was a hub of the coaching network with routes north, south, east and west. The celebrated George Inn has been a staging post for centuries, and had two waiting rooms for travellers. Also the town was part of the inland waterways system linked via the Stamford Canal which ran to Market Deeping and joined with the navigable Welland to the Wash.

Bridge Street looking towards the Welland Bridge

STAMFORD TOWN TRAIL

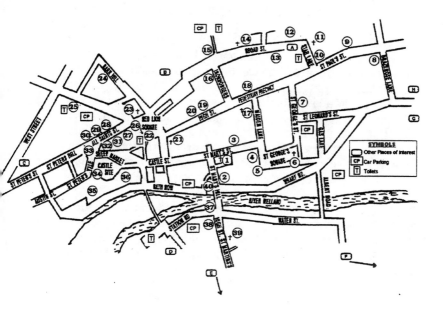

STAMFORD TOWN TRAIL

This route will take you through most of the old town and I have chosen "just" forty places of interest to whet the appetite for more. The route starts at St Mary's Church at the top of St Mary's Hill and not far from the river. It is easily accessible on foot from any of the Car Parks around the town. Allow yourself between one and two hours to complete the walk.

St Mary's Church [1] (13th to 15th centuries) is easily identified by its imposing broach spire and tower. Inside is a 14th century statue of the Virgin, a 15th century painted ceiling and 19th century stained glass and woodwork. Behind you on the corner of St Mary's Hill and St Mary's Place, is the *Georgian Town Hall [2]* completed in 1779 with the Stamford Borough coats of arms on each facade. Walking round the back of the church leads into St Mary's Street. Opposite is the former *Stamford Hotel [3]* with large Corinthian columns, Greek decoration and fine internal plaster work; it was converted to small shop units in 1983.

On the corner of St George's Square (at the south-eastern edge of the Danish borough of the 9th and 10th centuries) is the *Stamford Theatre and Arts Centre [4]* incorporating the Tourist Information Centre which is open most days. The complex has a good refreshment area and toilets. The Theatre was of Georgian construction built in 1768, it closed a hundred years later and was restored in 1978. Further into the Square are the *Assembly Rooms of 1727 [5]*, also now part of the Arts Centre. The latter has a room with a coved ceiling and decorated chimney breast. Other buildings of interest are Nos 14 to 20 though No 19 is not Georgian architecture.

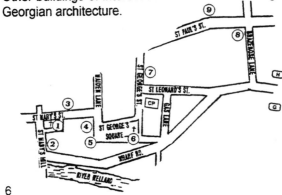

St George's Church [6] is associated with the Order of the Garter after William Bruges, first garter King of Arms who rebuilt the church in the 15th century. Only one window of 25 with mottoes and garters remains in the chancel. A Church has been on this site from 1199 and the present building was used by BBC Television for the Middlemarch production of 1993.

St George's Square

Walking northwards along St George's Street will take you past the medieval *Reedman's Court [7]* with a stone carved chain in the doorway. A plaque above the door reads:-

> *REEDMAN'S COURT. A LATE MEDIEVAL HALL HOUSE PARTLY REBUILT IN THE 1850'S AND 1982.*

Turning right into St Paul's Street leads the explorer past many Medieval cottages (now shops) towards the *Brazenose Arch [8]*, the doorknocker of which was removed to Oxford in the 19th Century to recall the rebellious students from that city who studied at Brazenose Hall from 1333 to 1336. It was the "Brazen Nosed" bull door handle from there which was eventually installed in what is now Brazenose College, Oxford. The present handle is a replica. At the crossroads is a plaque indicating that here stood St Paul's Gate, one of the seven main entrances to Stamford.

Returning to the town by the same route the traveller will pass *Stamford High School [9]* with its pelican on the nest symbol that represents Christ and "+ me spede" (Christ help me) the motto of William Browne merchant and benefactor of the town. A similar device can also be seen on Latham's Hospital in Oundle. Stamford School was founded in 1532 and one time occupied the 12th century St Paul's Church, which is now the School Chapel.

William Browne's motto on the gate of Stamford School.

On the corner with Star Lane is the *Half Moon Inn [10]* the earliest mention of which comes in 1744 but it was substantially rebuilt into its present form in 1938. Then comes the Stamford *United Reform Church [11]* built in 1819; turning into Broad Street, eleven houses of which date from the 17th and 18th centuries, on the corner are public toilets and the *Lord Burghley [12] public house* is across the road. Although there has been a building on the site since medieval times, this one dates from 1980! The area opposite was originally the Broad Street access to the butchers' market but eventually became Stamford's Museum in the same year, (see Appendix). Also visible is the former Congregational Hall (now URC) and a Mormon place of worship. The *Old Bakehouse [13]*, (now converted to studio apartments) is on the south side, then comes the Roman Catholic Church of *St Mary and St Augustine [14]* built in 1864 with a Gothic arcaded bell turret.

Narrow Newgates [15] which originally led to a postern gate, and Nags Head Passage (footpath) lead north to car parks and toilets on North Street. Turn left here down Ironmonger Street and note on the corner a *plaque [16]*:-

> *HERE FORMERLY STOOD THE MARKET CROSS TO WHICH SOME PRISONERS WERE BROUGHT FROM GAOL ON MARKET DAYS AND WHIPPED AROUND IT. IT WAS MENTIONED IN 1550 AND WAS TAKEN DOWN BY 1696*

Walk down the pedestrianised Ironmonger Street which has mainly 19th century shop fronts, and which will be filled with Market Stalls on a Friday and into the main pedestrian precinct of High Street with Georgian and Regency houses. Opposite the junction on the corner of Maiden Lane is the redundant *St Michael's Church [17]* which dates from the mid 1800's and converted into shops and offices in 1982 and further down the Lane is the King's Head public house. Across High Street is the *Public Library [18]* with massive Tuscan columns. This was originally an open portico built in 1804 giving access into the butchers' market. It was enclosed to form the Library in 1906.

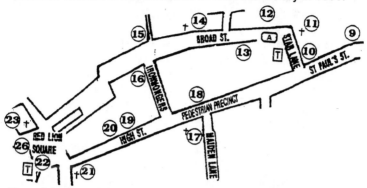

Turn right down High Street, (also with a Market on Fridays) past nationally known shops and many specialist independent ones, and notice the many passages such as Wellington Lane which lead off right and left to other attractive areas. One such goes down to the Black Bull Inn. The *Halifax building [19]* was rebuilt in 1982 and next door is *Gothic House [20]* with a Tudor style facade of the mid 1800's which houses Stamford's main bookshop, Walkers. The building dates from 15th or 16th century. Opposite is Lloyds Bank, 1880, in Italianate style, built for some curious reason of Portland and Bath limestone (which must have been brought in on the railway), rather than the local Barnack Rag(stone). Carvings depict four continents.

Pass on down the street; at the end to the left is *St John's Church [21]* built in 1451 in Perpendicular style. The medieval roofs have carved angel decorations and glass work was restored in 1974. The exterior tower is a staircase to an old roof loft.

Across the road is *Red Lion Square [22],* an early market area, which contained a poultry market in the 18th century, a butter market in the 19th and possibly a Guildhall and is reputed to have had a pillory. It now has a Market on a Saturday. There are toilets here.

Look to your right to see the spire of *All Saints' Church [23]*, in All Saints Place. With its Early English and Perpendicular style, it is mentioned in the Domesday Book. It has a 13th century Chancel and separate 15th century spire which stands at 152ft. The font is carved in Purbeck Marble from the Dorset coast (actually a limestone which can be polished) and the Reredos carving of the Last Supper is in Caen stone, from France.

Rebuilt in around 1645 by the prosperous Browne family of wool merchants of Calais, it includes a life-size bronze to William and Margaret Browne. He was Alderman of the borough six times between 1635 and 1670 and his motto "+ me spede" ("Christ help me") is visible in the chancel roof. (See also Stamford School [9])

Go past the church and up the hill to see *Barn Hill House [24]* on your left. This is Stamford's largest house, built in the 17th or 18th centuries, with a Neoclassical front added in 1843. It is probable that its garden is the site of St Clement's Church. On the other side of the road is the old Trinity Methodist chapel of 1804.

Turn left and go down to Scotgate, with the terracotta *Scotgate Inn [25]* at the junction built in the late 19th century with the heads of Hermes and Bacchus above the doors. Nearby are toilets and a Car Park. Also note the two hospitals (almshouses) Snowden's (or St John's Callis) 17th century, originally built to maintain seven poor widows of the town, the present building dates from the 1820's. Alongside is Truesdale's. Rebuilt in 1833 in grand Tudor-Gothic style it maintained eight men.

In All Saints Place is the Victorian *Post Office [26]* of 1896. The Place runs into All Saints' Street and two doors away is the *Mill Stone public house [27]* in existence from the early 18th century with the inscription on the frontage:-

> GOOD STABLING
> AND LOOSE BOXES

Near the corner of Scotgate and All Saints' Street is the *Stamford Brewery Museum [28]*. The museum frontage which displays the words MELBOURN BROTHERS was a commercial

10

concern from 1825 to 1974 when it was opened to the public. Next comes the Albion Tavern (previously named The Globe) and the then the next building has (in the same gothic script) ODD FELLOWS HALL; it was later converted to a *cinema [29]*. Then comes the wrought iron archway of *All Saints Mews [30]*.

Turn towards the castle area down *Mallory Lane [31]* - this ancient street has been here since before the 14th century; formerly lit with gas lamps these now contain long-life electric bulbs. Also note *St Peter's Callis [32]* (almshouses) dating from the 15th century at the corner of All Saints and Sheepmarket. *St Peter's Hill [33]* was constructed from the 17th to the 19th century. The Stamford Institution built in 1842, is in Greco-Egyptian style. The Sheepmarket was created in 1781 and the Golden Fleece pub has survived since the 1850's, its sign displays the emblem of the sheep trade.

In 1068 a Norman motte and bailey *Castle [34]* was constructed on the site of earlier defences. It was sometime owned by the baron who helped force the signing of Magna Carta and was an original William the Conqueror castle. The circular stone keep some sixty feet (19m) in diameter was excavated in 1933 and the castle mound removed in 1935; the area is now used as a Bus Station! Of the associated old town wall only *three arches plus walling in St Peter's Vale [35]* remain.

Either walk down Castle Dyke off Sheepmarket or one of several passages such as Olde Barn Passage from Castle Street and go down to the river via Bath Row to see the 1823 *Bath House [36]* The 1880 flood level mark is on the left. Then cross the river by the footbridge (see below).

If you should choose to view the shops you can still reach the river down St John's Lane, off St Mary's Street, (steep, cobbled and not wide enough for our umbrella on Midsummer's Day!). Walking back along Bath Row, cross the river by the footbridge to reach Station Road and walk towards the main river bridge with *almshouses [37]* to the left and the famous *George Hotel [38]* to the right.

Rear view of Lord Burghley's Hospital alongside the River Welland.

The long almshouses are Lord Burghley's Hospital. Established by the Benedictines in about 1175 as the Hospital of St Thomas and St John and administered by Peterborough Abbey. The archway and buttresses remain. Enlarged in the 15th century it was endowed by William Cecil (1520-1598) 1st Lord Burghley and further extended in the 17th century. The tall chimneys are 18th century and alterations were undertaken as late as 1964.

The George Hotel with its facade of 1724 fronting an early 17th century building has been a staging post for centuries and at one time had "York" and "London" waiting rooms for travellers going north and south. On display are the walking stick and portrait of Daniel Lambert who at one point weighed in at 52 stone 11 pounds (342 kg)! His walking stick is a section of a small tree; when he died his coffin took over 110 square feet of elm wood to construct. The George has a 14th century Screen and a crypt which is part of an original hospital of the Knights of St John of Jerusalem. (A military order dedicated to the protection of pilgrims to the Holy Land.).

At the junction of High Street St Martins, look right to see the road-wide gallows and *St Martin's Church [39]* built around 1470 in Late Perpendicular style with pinnacled tower. The church which was a favourite subject of artist Joseph Turner and writer Sir Walter Scott, contains the Burghley chapel and tombs,

12

and a large, marble and alabaster monument to William Cecil, 1st Lord Burghley. St Martin's is on the site of a fortress constructed by Edward, King of Wessex, in 918, and later a Norman church built by the

Facade of building in the High Street

Abbot of the Benedictine Monastery at Peterborough. The Grave of Daniel Lambert (see The George Hotel) is in the extended churchyard .

Head back to your starting point across the Town Bridge with its former Toll House. The Town Hall, demolished in 1776, once straddled the bridge. Walk up St Mary's Hill (formerly Briggate eg: Bridge Street). One shop nearby was originally a monastery which was destroyed in 1641 during the Civil war.

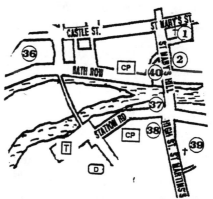

The buildings with timber framed overhangs date from the 17th century. The Norman arch at the entrance to *St Mary's Passage [40]* which leads back to Bath Row, is constructed of Stamford Marble and may have led to the Castle. Notice the plaque:-

> *THIS NORMAN ARCH IS BELIEVED TO BE ONE OF THE POSTERN GATES IN THE TOWN WALLS*

The Welland Bridge

Other places of interest in the area include:-

A   Stamford Museum in Broad Street is open all the year round, though not on Sundays from October to March, Life-size models of Daniel Lambert and "General" Tom Thumb are on display together with the history of the town through two millennia.

B   Browne's Hospital, founded c.1480 by merchant William Browne as almshouses. It was rebuilt in 1870 but retained the 15th century chapel and glass work and Jacobean Hall. Floor marks still show positioning of sleeping cubicles. It has a recent clock tower and monuments to servicemen killed in two world wars and Malaya in 1955. Of particular interest is the Warden's house with its bay window overhanging the pavement.

Other Almshouses in the town are the 17th century Williamson's and the 18th century Hopkins' in St Peter's Street and Fryer's from the 19th century in Kettering Road.

C   The Bastion Tower in West Street is the best remaining part of the old Town Wall from Norman times.

D   Stamford Railway Station, built in 1848 in Tudor style with a pierced turret, for the Midland Railway. When the station was opened near the river and the George Inn, the latter opened a special entrance to receive guests from the railway opposite.

E   Wothorpe House, built by the Cecil family and now a partly dismantled ruin visible to the southwest. Nearer views can be had from the Garden Centre in Wothorpe hamlet but the ruins are dangerous and should not be approached.

F   Burghley House, largely Elizabethan, this grand house has been the home of the Exeter and Cecil families for 400 years. Built between 1565 and 1587 on the site of a 12th century Monastery by William Cecil, advisor to Queen Elizabeth I, and Lord High Treasurer of England who later became 1st Lord Burghley. It has a central courtyard with rounded turreted corner towers and three differing facades show various Italianate styles. The house was bombarded and stormed by William the Conqueror in 1643.

In the house there are eighteen State, thirty-five main and over eighty lesser rooms. The Great Hall has a large fireplace and a double hammerbeam roof. Carved woodwork is by Grinling Gibbons (see also Exton) and there are sumptuous wall paintings by the artist Antonio Verrio in the "Heaven" and "Hell" rooms.

Successive members of the Cecil family have added to the collection of over many hundreds of great works of art including paintings, Japanese ceramics, European porcelain and earthenware, marble sculptures, exquisite furniture and tapestries. John Cecil (1648-1700), the 5th Earl, collected over 300 important paintings whilst touring the continent, particularly in Italy.

An imposing west gateway (originally intended as the main entrance) leads into the property, which is just twenty minutes walk from the centre of Stamford. Through the Deer Park which is surrounded by a three-mile wall, and which was laid out by Capability Brown in the 18th century, there are many walks through avenues of trees. The herd of Fallow deer have been here since the 1500's. The Orangery (also designed by Brown) has been converted into a restaurant offering rest and refreshment in the charming surroundings of rose beds and gardens. World famous Horse Trials are held in the Park each September. The Roman Road, Ermine Street, crosses the southern part of the Park.

The House is open from Easter to early October, during the mid part of each day, it is viewable by guided tour only, except on Sundays when there are guides in each room. The only exception is that the house is not open to visitors on the Saturday of the Horse Trials.

G   St Leonard's Priory, (under restoration), in Priory Road contains a Benedictine cell from c.1080; though the priory was founded in the 7th century by Wilfrid, tutor to the son of the Saxon king, Oswy. Later the site belonged to Durham Abbey. There are splendid arches on the west front and arcades on the northern wall together with late Norman carvings inside.

H   Whitefriars Gateway, a 14th century part of the White Friary and now the entrance to Stamford Hospital. It is the only

remaining part of the House of the White Friars in which Richard
II held a council, and in which Queen Elizabeth I stayed in 1565.

For more information I can recommend the Stamford Museum's
and Lincolnshire County Council's excellent trails covering
various aspects such as chimneys or Georgian architecture. At
less than £1.00 each the visitor is recommended to buy them all!
They can be purchased from the Tourist Information Centre,
Walker's Bookshop and many other local stores. Also
recommended are other books which can be found listed in the
Bibliography at the back, many of which are still in print.

THE AREA SOUTH AND WEST OF THE A1

Barnsdale, Barrowden, Collyweston, Duddington and Tixover
Edith Weston, Empingham, Exton, Fineshade Abbey, Ketton
(with Aldgate and Geeston), Kings Cliffe, Normanton,
North Luffenham, Rutland County, Rutland Water, South
Luffenham, Thornhaugh, Tickencote, Tinwell, Wakerley,
Wakerley Woods, Wansford, Nene Valley Railway, Whitwell,
Wittering and Southorpe

BARNSDALE. SK912107

This is the Barnsdale of TV gardener Geoff Hamilton; sadly missed by thousands of enthusiasts to whom he conveyed his dynamic love of gardening. The Viking Way leads north from Barnsdale Lodge at SK908094 along the tree-lined Barnsdale Avenue towards Exton. One mile from the junction is the famous TV garden. The family nursery, Barnsdale Plants, and the next door show gardens are open to the public.

Surprisingly, the infamous outlaw, Robin Hood and his followers camped in the Barnsdale Forest at some point in their career. There is access to Rutland Water here with a large car-park, public conveniences and picnic areas. Also here a Drought Garden and Arboretum.

BARROWDEN SP944999

It seems likely that there has been a settlement here since around 500 AD. At the time of the Domesday Book the manor belonged to the King. The Jurassic Way passes through the village along the Morcott and Wakerley roads and crosses a disused railway line and the Welland River. A slight variation of the Way conveys the walker across the river via a footbridge and on towards Wakerley. The village was not "enclosed" until the 1880's and the village green and duck pond are traditional features. Near the pond are a manor house, and the Exeter

Arms inn.

Down Church Lane is the Church of St Peter built from locally quarried stone. It is 13th century with 14th century west tower; the east window and the enlarged clerestory date from 15th century and there is 19th century chancel roof. Especially prominent is a large wall monument on the north wall to "Roland Digby, Rector of Barrowden" who died in 1546 and who is buried in the churchyard. There a statue to Our Lady of Walsingham on the sill of a north aisle window. On the wall of a cottage in Church Lane is an odd carved stone which has obviously been sawn off on its right hand edge.

| COLLYWESTON | SK996028 |

Up until the 14th century the village was just "Weston", becoming Colyn's Weston in 1331. (Colin being a short form of Nicholas, after Sir Nicholas de Segrave, Lord of the Manor, Governor of Northampton Castle and Marshall of England). The manor was later sold to the Tryon family, (see Bulwick in 'Exploring Oundle and Surrounding Villages'), in 1650 although there has been no lord of the manor since the 18th century. The manor house was moved to its present site in the early 20th century, possibly to improve the view! Iron Age and Roman relics have been found nearby, and The Drove is a Roman Road to Wansford.

The church here is the 13th century St Andrew The Apostle, rebuilt in the 15th partly of Barnack Rag and partly of rubble. The tower has pinnacles some seven metres high. Church Gate Cottage has a sundial with "I Stay For No Man" inscribed above.

Opposite is Blue Bell House which may have been an inn at one time. "The Old Forge", on the main road has a giant horse-shoe over its garage and on Back Lane, but visible only on foot (from what is probably private land) is a giant curved sundial standing some four metres high. To the west of the

The Old Forge

village are ancient fish ponds. The remaining inn is The Cavalier.

On the Easton on the Hill road which overlooks Wittering airfield there is a disused and overgrown windmill. During WW2 this part was originally Collyweston airfield, but the two were joined in about 1943 by one long runway. The village was strafed and bombed in 1940 and 1941 by enemy aircraft.

The road to Ketton descends 60m (200ft) into the Welland valley and crosses a six arched bridge into the gratefully restored county of Rutland. The bridge, which was repaired thanks to a bequest in 1576, has curved arches on the Rutland side and pointed ones on the Northants. The "Jurassic Way" runs through the area and intersects the road just before the bridge.

The Welland Bridge

Collyweston Slate was quarried in the parish. Actually it is not slate but thin sheets of limestone. At one time every farmer would have had a small pit on his land to recover the stone which was then soaked with water and left out in the open. Winter weather would then split it along natural lines by frost action. The sheets would then be "dressed" (trimmed to roughly rectangular shape) and eventually hung by a single peg on wooden laths across a roof. Few workmen have the skill today and their craft is in high demand and as demand exceeds the supply, old slates are now re-dressed and re-hung.

Today the Collyweston quarry, locally known as "The Deeps", contains grassland with various species of grass and downy oak. The area is managed by the Northamptonshire Trust for Nature Conservation, (see also Easton on the Hill).

DUDDINGTON AND TIXOVER SK987008

The Royal Oak is a favourite place for relaxation. The village has a Manor House, a number of wells and a weir on the River Welland. The packhorse bridge (shown on the cover of Landranger map No 141) across the valley, near the old watermill dated 1664, once carried the A47 before it was re-routed. The Jurassic Way passes by and there are rights of way to Kings Cliffe and Tixover.

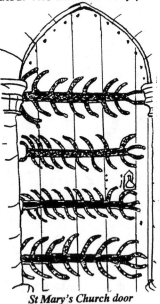
St Mary's Church door

The church of St Mary is 12th century or earlier and the door is worked with a fishbone design in ironwork. This the original door from around 1220, constructed to provide protection against forced entry. Most medieval churches have their tower at the west end of the nave; St Mary's tower is at the southeast corner, probably because of the way the land slopes steeply down to the river.

Inside the church are traces of medieval wall paintings, a 13th century font and a 17th century communion table. Also visible are many monuments to the Jackson family of Stamford who owned the estate and built the Manor House. Nearby is a cottage which was the parish workhouse until 1834. The village was

20

machine-gunned in an enemy aircraft attack in 1940.

Tixover is a short drive from Duddington and has a single street alongside the River Welland. On the banks of the river and half a mile from the present dwellings, in a walled cemetery, the church of St Luke has a Norman tower and the interior arch is c.1140. Medieval stone seats line the chancel walls and there is old glass and woodwork. There is a 17th century monument to the Lord of the Manor.

EASTON ON THE HILL   TF011047

The Glebe House was home of Capt. Lancelot Skynner circa 1775. He was lost when the HMS Lutine foundered on the Dutch coast in 1799. The salvaged Lutine Bell now hangs in Lloyds and is rung to mark the loss of a vessel. Over the front door is a large sundial with "Fear The Lord Always" inscribed above. (Please note this is private property, though visible from the road). Nearby is The "Priest's House" which has variously been a rectory and a stable. Now it is National Trust Property and houses a museum of village collectables.

There is a ruined windmill visible from the main road overlooking the Wittering airfield. Many of the properties date from the mid-17th century, though the Old Coach House is 1839. Public Houses are The Exeter Arms (restaurant only) and The Oak Inn on the main Stamford Road. The latter serves good food and is recommended. The Blue Bell Inn near the war memorial is more of a "local" and does not offer food.

The 13th century Church of All Saints stands in a large churchyard 285 feet above sea level, overlooking the Welland Valley. Although dating from the 12th century much of the structure was rebuilt in the next and added to in the 14th. The tower was built in the 15th century and is 100 ft. high. The church contains two stone screens and a George IV memorial from 1820. The interior has been restored and whitewashed and fragments of wall paintings were discovered in 1951. The sundial over the south porch is dated 1791. The rectory is Georgian.

"The Deeps" is Collyweston Quarry, (nearer to Easton than Collyweston) now a nature reserve operated by the Northants Wildlife Trust on lease form the Burghley estate. With around 200 species recorded it is a Site of Special Scientific Interest. Rights of way run along the Ketton Drift track and to Tinwell and the Hereward/Jurassic Way passes through.

EDITH WESTON   SK927054

The village is on the southeast corner of Rutland Water. Edith was Queen to Edward the Confessor and this part of Rutland was given to her. A nearby road is King Edward's way. Much of the community's water came from a single pump at the turn of the 20th century.

The church is the 12th century St Mary the Virgin with Norman carving and a one-handed clock. Lundon Hall to the southwest has connections with Gilbert White of Selborne. Within the parish, at Rutland Water are a sailing club, picnic areas, a fishing lodge, public conveniences and a nature reserve, (see Rutland Water).

EMPINGHAM SK951085

On the River Gwash, a village with a population of five hundred even in the Domesday Book. With twelve mills, it was once part of the Normanton Park estate. In 1764 Sir Gilbert Heathcote forcibly moved the entire population of Normanton to here to improve his view from Normanton Hall, leaving only the church of St Matthew and the Hall standing!

Manorial Coat of Arms

Several of the buildings in the main street, including some attractive red and white stone cottages, carry the manorial crest. Many houses date from around the 16th and 17th centuries.

"Yeomans" is dated 1691. The White Horse Inn is a popular watering hole and offers quality accommodation. Church bridge (SK951084) was a packhorse crossing originally. Twice damaged by floods in the 19th century It was widened in the late 1950's. On the Post Office is a reminder of days when banks as we now know them were not accessible to all:

```
MONEY ORDER OFFICE
AND
POST OFFICE
SAVINGS BANK
```

The church of St Peter is early English with a 14th century slender crocketed spire with the tower dated 1713. Inside are fragments of mural paintings and a small amount of stained glass. The west front is notable. Adjacent to it is Prebendal House, with magnificent gates, sometime summer palace to the Bishops of Lincoln. In a nearby field is a dovecote of seven hundred boxes, (SK955089). (See also Pickworth and Losecoat Field).

Further along the road are Roadside Verge Nature Reserves managed by the County Council to preserve wildlife. The river Gwash, dammed to make Rutland Water, flows south of the village and rises near to old fish ponds.

The church of St Peter and St Paul dates from the 13th and 14th centuries and stands remote from the village, (SK921113), in Exton Park, the grounds of Exton Hall. Much restoration was done in the 19th century after severe storm damage in 1843. Inside is an ostentatious monument to Baptist Noel, third Viscount Campden, Lord Lieutenant of Rutland. Made of white and black marble the largest is perhaps fifteen foot high and twelve across. It is the work of Grinling Gibbons and it dominates the building. There are several other smaller examples throughout the church, two by the renowned sculptor, Nollekins, whose name is chiselled into the marble.

The adjacent Exton Hall was destroyed by fire in 1810 though the bleached remains are still in place. A few hundred feet away is the magnificent rebuilt hall, completed in 1851. Also visible from the churchyard is a lake and summerhouse. There are footpaths through the grounds and a map is available from The Fox and Hounds Inn. Hawkswell Spring is at the south edge of the village the Viking Way traverses the village before going northeast and north to Greetham with its falconry centre and golf club.

Summerhouse at Exton Hall

The Inn on the Village Green provided two weary researchers with welcome appetizing sustenance on a cold February day. And the sweet course came for free! Across the road from the pub and next to the war memorial is a private house with "R.KIMSEY—DRUGGIST" over the door. There are Rights of way to the Cottesmore Road; to Fort Henry (see below) and the site of medieval Horn; to Whitwell on the banks of Rutland Water.

Horn House is built on the site of the medieval village of Horn at SK954116, alongside the valley of the North Brook. Fort Henry is a summer house in the grounds, dating from 1785 on the "shore" of the upper of two lakes formed by a dam across the Brook. Designed by the architect William Legg of Stamford it can only be reached on foot or horseback through the Exton Estates land from Greetham, Exton Horn Mill or the A1. On the Exton to Tickencote road directly south of Horn House and nearby Empingham Old Wood is Horn Mill Trout Farm at SK953105.

FINESHADE ABBEY　　　SP973977

On the site of the medieval Augustinian Priory of St Mary and opposite the site of Castle Hymel, this was the Norman castle house of the Engayne family and the long curved bank marks the outer edge of the bailey, (see Appendix: Motte & Bailey). The castle was demolished around the 13th century to found the priory and that remained until the dissolution of the monasteries in 1536. Ten years later Sir Roger Kirkham of Warmington bought it and converted it to a house. Again demolished in the 18th century it was replaced by a Georgian mansion which remains substantially intact today.

Finshade Abbey

The Jurassic Way passes through the woods. Other Rights of way are south to Blatherwycke and Laxton, east to Kings Cliffe and north to Top Lodge in Fineshade Wood where there is parking, a Caravan Club site and cyclists may ride in the woods without charge including the use of a specially designed mountain bike trail. The wood is home to Muntjac and Fallow deer and several species of butterfly.

A tributary of the Welland, the River Chater (from which the village derives its name) flows past the architecturally superb Early English 12th to the 14th century, St Mary's Church. (The drawing cannot do it justice - visit it yourself!) The church has an impressive central tower, a spire built of Barnack stone and a Norman font. Aisles were added in 13th century; the chancel was rebuilt in the 19th century and the panelled roof restored in medieval design and colours.

Opposite is a large building known as "The Priory" with a garden occasionally open for viewing. Down the road "The Railway" inn has an attractive sign outside and there is another Inn, The Northwick Arms.

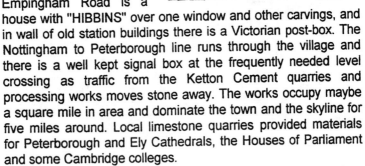

St Mary's Church, Ketton

At the corner of Empingham Road is a house with "HIBBINS" over one window and other carvings, and in wall of old station buildings there is a Victorian post-box. The Nottingham to Peterborough line runs through the village and there is a well kept signal box at the frequently needed level crossing as traffic from the Ketton Cement quarries and processing works moves stone away. The works occupy maybe a square mile in area and dominate the town and the skyline for five miles around. Local limestone quarries provided materials for Peterborough and Ely Cathedrals, the Houses of Parliament and some Cambridge colleges.

Aldgate and Geeston are related hamlets on the south side of the Chater. For details on the bridge on the Ketton to Collyweston road please see under Collyweston. The Empingham road is intersected by the Hereward Way footpath. On the Ketton to Edith Weston road there is a Cross Country Course in Ketton Park; and on the outskirts a derelict windmill.

Beware the level crossing as the main line from Peterborough runs through the village.

As its name implies the village was a Royal Manor, one of three bailiwicks of Rockingham Forest but its medieval market fell into disuse with the passage of time. The village was all but razed to the ground by Roundheads in the civil war. Almshouses are dated 1668. A sundial (1686) commemorates William Law the religious writer and town benefactor. The inscription reads

"BOOKS OF PIETY ARE HERE LENT TO ANY PERSONS OF THIS OR ENY NEIGHBOURING TOWNS"

All Saints and St James' Church

The dominant building material is Collyweston stone. The church is All Saints and St James, it has a Norman tower and 13th century spire. Some fragments of stained glass from Fotheringhay are visible. The Church Room was once part of the water mill and the Willow Brook still flows beneath. Contained within are village archives and photographs of a bygone age.

The Old Red Lion Inn, (in private hands), still has a metal AA sign on the wall showing distances to various local towns. The Cross Keys public house has that sign carved on the outside. It is dated 1732 but thought to be older. There are springs and wells in the village and to the south approachable on foot is "The Spa" an ancient mineral water source. The Manor House frontage situated on Main Street is early 17th century with older parts elsewhere and a 19th century staircase. Many other buildings date from the 18th and 19th centuries.

There was a USAAF base here during the second World War

with 1,400 personnel and almost 15,000 flights were recorded. An unusual memorial to the base personnel, with a stone replica of the wings of a P-51, a Spitfire and the twin-boom P-38, surrounded by unit badges may be seen on the Wansford Road which follows the line of an old Roman Road and there is an Equestrian Centre in the woodland of the Bedford Purlieus.

NORMANTON   SK933064

Southwest of Empingham is the drowned village of Normanton. In the mid 18th century Sir Gilbert Heathcote forcibly moved the entire population of the village to Empingham to improve his view from Normanton Hall!

After that only the Hall and the church of St. Matthew remained. The latter now sits on a promontory at the southeast corner of Rutland Water. Built by the Heathcote family it was partly demolished in 1911 and finally deconsecrated in 1970. Reopened as the Normanton Church Museum in 1984 it contains details about the construction of Rutland Water and a well-preserved Anglo-Saxon skeleton found nearby. Open from 11.00am to 4.00pm during April to September, a small charge is made for entry.

NORTH LUFFENHAM   SK934033

An entrance to North Luffenham Hall is through an arched gateway; another has an octagonal "gatehouse" alongside. On the end wall of a cottage opposite are three carved faces. Several of the houses date from the mid 17th century, and some are obviously estate cottages built to the same pattern. There are two inns, The Horse and

North Luffenham Hall Arch

Panniers and The Fox and Hounds. There is also more modern housing.

The church of St John the Baptist from 13th and 14th century though a list of rectors dates back to 1206. Tiling on the chancel floor appears to be a Victorian addition and there is a wooden model of the church from 1976. Traces of medieval wall paintings and glass are visible. In the churchyard are over forty war graves; members of the RAF, RAAF; RCAF; RNZAF and Royal Artillery.

A number of springs rise in the village. At SK928033 is a moat and there is a caravan site at the northern edge of the village. Rights of way towards Morcott. The road to South Luffenham crosses the River Cater by way of Moor Lane Bridge.

North Luffenham also gives its name to the RAF airfield which lies between the two Luffenhams. The airfield has been in use since 1940 when it was a bomber base with over 2000 personnel, (see also Woolfox Lodge).

RUTLAND COUNTY

The smallest county in England, named "Roteland" because of its red soil, was swallowed up by Leicestershire in the 1974 boundary changes. On 1st April 1997, after much lobbying by residents, the government of the day saw fit to reinstate it as a separate county. Only twenty miles across, the charm of England's "green and pleasant land" has rarely been better seen in such a small area. The county's motto is "Multum in Parvo" - Much in Little.

Edward the Confessor gave "Roteland" to his wife Eadgyth whose name lives on in the village of Edith Weston on the southeast corner of Rutland Water. The area had Royal ownership until the 16th century.

This man made lake of over 3000 acres was constructed in the 1970s and the village of Lower Hambleton was a casualty of the flooding of the Gwash Valley. There are numerous parking places around the lake

Normanton Church Museum

and adjacent to the village of Edith Weston there is a sailing club, a fishing lodge, cycle hire, picnic areas, public conveniences and the Normanton Church Museum. A small charge is made for parking.

Twenty five miles of footpaths and cycle tracks, (six of which are on the Hambleton peninsula - an un-flooded hill top), surround the lake perimeter, mostly off-road including across the dam. Many facilities are provided for the disabled, including an anglers' pontoon on the eastern tip of the peninsula.

The Rutland Belle

Just south of Whitwell Village is the deepest part of the lake and sea and diving ducks can often be seen. The Rutland Water Resource Centre is in the village at SK926081. There is parking at Sykes Lane with cycle hire, a Butterfly and Aquatic Centre with a walk through jungle with free-flying birds and butterflies, and a nature trail. Plus a picnic site, tourist information and public conveniences. Water sports include wind-surfing, canoeing plus trout and pike fishing at Whitwell Creek, with over sixty hire boats available. The "Rutland Belle" passenger cruiser embarks from here and at Normanton Church, (water levels permitting), and has been on the lake over ten years carrying over 300,000 passengers on her 45 minute round-trip cruise between May and September.

The western edge of the lake has an important bird-watching centre, whilst the northern "coast" has a nature reserve of 450 acres. Over 250 species of bird have been recorded including ospreys which are regular visitors. Upwards of 20,000 wildfowl are sometimes on the lake. Also here is an arboretum and a Drought Garden created by TV gardener, Geoff Hamilton, which aims to show ways in which gardens can be maintained without artificial watering.

There are a number of eating places around the Lake including the Normanton Park Hotel converted from the stables of Normanton Hall; the North Fishing Lodge and the Whitwell Harbour bar.

| **SOUTH LUFFENHAM** | SK942020 |

On the tributary of River Chater the road to North Luffenham crosses the river to the North. The church is St Mary the Virgin, yet another with no tower or spire, accessible via a footpath beside "The Chantry"; probably the old rectory. On the main Stamford Road is "The Halfway House" inn and opposite the church, "The Boot and Shoe". On the end wall of a related building, opposite the churchyard, is a plaque:

| *SAPCOTES CHARITY BEQUEATHED 1859 RESTORED 1901* |

Just outside the village is a windmill ruin from the 1830's. Rights of way west to Pilton, south-west Morcott and south-east to Barrowden.

Next to the church of St Andrew is the large and magnificent old rectory. The churchyard must have been very peaceful when established, and has two seats to allow rest and contemplation. Sadly, the village is near to the ever noisy A1 trunk road and the aircraft from the Wittering RAF base were constantly overhead when I visited. There is a right of way across the fields to Wittering.

Outside the Old School House is a drinking fountain (not in use) dated 1839. Also in the village is an old bakery, now a private house and a Manor House at the crossroads. Nearby is the site of the medieval village of Sibberton. Thornhaugh Hall (private property) on the road towards the A47 has intricate ironwork gates, and an ornamental lake with an arched bridge, visible from the road. Along the same road is a recent seat bearing a plaque:

"TO COMMEMORATE VE AND VJ DAY 1995 AND 50 YEARS OF PEACE"

TICKENCOTE   SK990095

A picturesque village situated on the River Gwash and alongside the Great North Road (A1) there are a few cottages and a farm, plus a Mill and Mill Cottage; many of the properties belong to Tickencote Estates. The Vinery has a large ornamental lake which can be seen from a seat in the churchyard. At the end of the village is The Old School House.

St Peter's Tickencote

The exterior of the church of St Peter has elegant carvings and the building dates from the 12th century and has a monastic feel. A gigantic Norman archway of six orders (concentric arches), each carved with different designs, leads into the chancel with its sexpartite vaulting with zigzag designs and a rare Norman boss. This is almost unique in England; only Canterbury Cathedral and Lincoln Minster have something similar. Restored at the instruction of Eliza Wingfield in the 1792 there are also carvings of crowned heads and bears. Equally rare is a Priest's Chamber running the whole length of the chancel but now only accessible through the vestry ceiling, the steps having been removed at the restoration. There is a 13th century Font and a 14th century wooden effigy of a knight in armour. An original pre-reformation bell now stands in a frame in the main aisle.

Rights of way lead to Tickencote Lodge Farm and Empingham. On the Tickencote to Exton road directly south of Horn House and nearby Empingham Old Wood is Horn Mill Trout Farm at SK953105, astride the North Brook.

The Old Forge, Tinwell

TINWELL   TF006063

On the western outskirts of Stamford near to the A1 junction. We had a good meal at The Crown Inn which boasts four pentanque (boule) courts. Very few buildings in the village are older than the 19th century and many belong to the Burghley Estate. Particularly worth a visit is the Old Forge and Shop (1848). Still used for its original purpose, and open all year, orders are taken for "one-off" ironwork. You can see a Victorian post box on the wall, and the main doors are surrounded by a gigantic stonework horseshoe.

The church of All Saints is unusual in having a saddle-back tower, and its clock was restored in 1964. The old rectory is now a hotel and there is a large manor house. Visible on the skyline to the south is All Saints, Easton on the Hill. There is a bridleway to Easton and a right of way follows the River Welland into Stamford.

St John The Baptist

The church of St John the Baptist has been declared redundant but has not been deconsecrated. It contains a carved Norman cancel arch and 15th century tower. Remote from the village, it probably marks the original centre of population. At the entrance is a Gate of Remembrance to the fallen and wounded of the 1914-1918 War.

The manor was bought in the 17th century by Sir Richard Cecil whose descendants still occupy Burghley Hall at Stamford. He laid out gardens which are usually open to the public one day per year.

The five arched span across the Welland was originally a packhorse bridge built in the mid 14th century to give access to the market at Barrowden. The bridge was widened at the instigation of Henry Cecil, Earl of Exeter in the late 18th century and the Exeter Arms inn, commemorates his name and coat of arms. There are Rights of way to Barrowden and Fineshade Abbey.

WAKERLEY WOODS   SP9698

As with Old Sulehay, these woods are a remnant of Rockingham forest which once covered a vast tract of central England. The trees are a mix of spruce, pine and larch and there is parking (a small charge is levied) and public conveniences, forest trails, an orienteering course and waymarked bridleways. Spanhoe Airfield (SP9497) is to the west. Built for the USAAF 8th Air Force it opened in 1943 and was closed for military flying in 1947. It is still used for light aviation, (see Appendix).

WANSFORD TL074993

Famous for its twelve arched bridge across the Nene, the seven most northerly arches were finished in 1577 and the others added up to 1795. The village now sits at the north-south and east-west crossroads junction of the main A47 and A1. The former county boundary between Huntingdonshire and Cambridgeshire is marked by a cast iron "milestone" in the centre of the bridge.

St Mary's, Wansford

There is a picnic site on the River Nene. An unnamed Roman Road runs from the village to Kings Cliffe. Nearby is the Sacrewell Farm and Country Centre (TF080003) accessed from the A47 just east of its junction with the A1 with a camp site, a working museum, a watermill dating from 1755, gardens and a nature trail, (see also under Sacrewell). Hostelries in the village include the famous Haycock Inn with its petanque area and the Cross Keys and Paper Mills public houses, with restaurants. There are also a number of shops including several selling antiques.

Various interesting buildings from 15th to 17th century are to be seen; one house, with parking outside, bears a plaque saying:

"PLEASE CHECK YOUR CAR FOR CATS"

The gatehouse to Stibbington House is on the Elton to Wansford road just as the village begins. It is an unique structure with a spired tower as well as more usual features. The church of St Mary the Virgin was, until the addition of a chancel in the early 20th century, the smallest in England. Tastefully decorated with excellent embroidery and whitewashed walls, it has a reputedly Saxon window in the bell tower, and a carved lectern.

To the east of the Nene is the hamlet of **Sutton**. Wansford

35

Station is closer to Sibson than Wansford and is the home of the Nene Valley Railway, the old Barnwell station has been rebuilt here. On the hills to the west is Sibson airfield; a popular place for parachuting and light aviation, it has two grass runways.

NENE VALLEY RAILWAY   TL094979

This is a seven and a half mile stretch of standard gauge track between Peterborough and Yarwell Junction. Mainly a volunteer railway, with very few paid staff, it was once part of the Blisworth, Northampton and Peterborough Railway. The first passenger train ran in 1845 and the next year the line was incorporated into the LNWR (London and North Western Railway). At one time there was a link to Birmingham via Yarwell Junction and Seaton. One hundred and twenty years later all services had ceased except for some quarry freight traffic and the occasional "Oundle School Special". BR closed the line in 1972.

Wansford Station

However, Peterborough was a Development Area and many enthusiasts mourned the loss of the branch lines. A Railway Society began in 1970 and with the help of the Development Corporation who bought and leased the line, the NVR was formed. As it came late onto the scene in respect of acquiring British equipment, rolling stock has been drawn from many continental sources requiring some modification of lineside equipment to accommodate the different loading gauge. A missing section of track was re-laid and the Wansford Steam Centre opened at Easter 1974.

Much more volunteer work was done over the next three years including moving the old Barnwell wooden station building (1884) to platform 2 and the opening of the line to public services from Wansford to Orton Mere in June 1977. The 1930's Turntable was originally in Peterborough and was extended to take any of the NVR's rolling stock when moved to its present site. The extension to Peterborough through the recently opened Nene Park was completed in 1985 and opened by HRH Prince Edward on June 30 1986.

Wansford Station is headquarters of the NVR, the Signal Box is from 1907 and the yard is home to a large collection of locomotives and coaches including an ex-LMS Black 5 No 5231 and a main line class diesel D306; a Swedish 2-6-2T No 1178; a Polish State Railways 2-10-0 No 7173; a B.R. Class 5 4-6-0 No 73050; French Compound 4-6-0 No 3-628; Danish F Class 0-6-0T No 656 and 2-6-4T No 745. Rolling stock includes some ex Southern Railways air-braked and Danish coaches. Also of note is "Thomas" a tank engine named by the Rev W. Awdry and bedecked in Thomas the Tank Engine livery. He has a number of special days throughout the year - but usually takes his holidays in September!!

Trains run most weekends from April to October, on some weekdays in the summer months and on special occasions. A typical journey will run from Wansford to Peterborough via Ferry Meadows and Orton Mere, first through the tunnel to Yarwell junction then back to the Peterborough NVR Station (just 20 minutes from the town centre by footpath). Passengers may join and alight anywhere except at Yarwell and timetables and details of travel are available from the Wansford Booking Office and shop or from Tourist Information Centres. Also at Peterborough is Railworld (not NVR) with a large model railway and several themed displays such as Rail and the Environment and Local Rail History. Please note: The original mock-Tudor station on platform 3 is privately owned and not open to the public.

| WHITWELL | SK925087 |

A small village on the A606, the "Rutland Belle" cruiser plies the waters of Rutland Water from here and the main rescue centre for the lake is in Whitwell Creek. A large recreational area by the water has a water sports area, a restaurant, cycle hire and many other facilities. The church on the main road has a bell cote with two bells. The Inn is the Noel Arms commemorating one of Rutland's illustrious families, (see also Exton).

WITTERING AND SOUTHORPE   TF056020

On a tributary of the River Nene, the Church of All saints has a Saxon chancel arch and a bell in the tower commemorating those lost in WW2. The cemetery contains over seventy war graves; mainly of RAF personnel though there are also graves of Canadian and New Zealand nationals plus those of the RNVR and RAFVR.

This is the main UK base for Harrier V/STOL "jump jets". The Gate Guardian is a Harrier F3. The base lies partly in Cambridgeshire with the western half in Rutland. Housing for the RAF airfield and its infrastructure dominates the village: one pub is the Phoenix. There is an English Catholic Church and on the road from the A47, and equestrian centre. Rights of way west to Thornhaugh and Barnack. **Southorpe** is a nearby village to the south consisting mainly of a farming community.

THE AREA EAST OF THE A1 AND SOUTH OF THE A16

Bainton with Ashton, Barnack with Pilsgate, Helpston, Maxey, Sacrewell, Stibbington and Water Newton, Ufford, Upton, West Deeping, Wothorpe on the Hill.

BAINTON WITH ASHTON   TF094061

Bainton Crossroads

At the main crossroads is the church of St Mary and a stone ball surmounts a massive "pyramid" of stone steps. Also at the junction with the Tallington Road is a short avenue of old trees and at the time of writing, an old-style illuminated "STOP" sign with the inverted triangle. Within the parish, but on the north-south Roman King Street are fisheries set in old gravel workings. As this is the start of the Fens the road crosses over the Maxey Cut and associated water courses at the six Lolham Bridges. A right of way leads to Helpston.

Ashton is a charming hamlet in rich arable land to the southeast through which runs the Torpel Way, (see Appendix Four). The road to Tallington crosses the railway on a wide level crossing, and the gate keeper's cottage is dated 1848.

BARNACK WITH PILSGATE   TF079051

The village is first recorded in the Anglo Saxon Chronicle as Beornica and the in the Domesday Book as Bernac. Many local houses and churches are built of "Barnack Rag"; limestone quarried in the parish until the end of the 15th century. Charles ·

Kingsley lived here in the 1820's before moving to Devon.

On the western outskirts of this large village is a nature reserve created from the old quarry workings, "Barnack Holes and Hills" were a favourite place for the naturalist poet, John Clare (see Helpston). Twenty eight species of butterfly and nine of wild orchids can be found here. On warm summer evenings glowing fireflies can be seen darting amongst the trees. There are wells and springs in the village. Pubs in the village include The Millstone which is open long hours and offers food and The Fox with limited opening. Opposite the church is Cedar House with a fine example of cast-iron railings and a magnificent specimen of its namesake towering above the property and visible from the churchyard.

The Church is St John the Baptist; inside is a seated figure of Christ in Majesty and an English leaved font. The screen is ornately carved and painted and the ceiling magnificently painted. The tower is Saxon dating from c1020 and the spire one of the earliest in the country. Every century since has seen additions to the structure and it has been a place of worship for a thousand years. In use today, it gives the visitor the feeling of a place well cared for and dedicated to the glory of God. In the outside wall of a garden in the village is an archway which once stood between the tower and nave.

The grave of George Ayscouth Booth in the church of St John The Baptist, Barnack.

In the churchyard is a unique grave with an amazing example of the stone-mason's craft. On top of the grave is a fallen palm tree with intricately carved palm fronds.

The dedication reads to:

GEORGE AYSCOUTH BOOTH
GENTLEMAN CADET R M C SANDHURST
1847-1862

Tower Windmill on the Pilsgate to Wittering road is disused but still has its sails. **Pilsgate** is to the north west but within Barnack parish. The Pilsgate Lodges are at the northern entrance to Burghley Park. Further towards the A1, Walcot Hall dates from 1678. In Pilsgate itself is the delightfully named Puddingbag Lane. Rights of way to the west join the Hereward Way; to the south down Church Lane towards Walcot and Ufford.

The Clare Memorial

| **HELPSTON** | TF123056 |

Birthplace of John Clare the poet (1793-1864). He is buried in the churchyard of St Botolph, approached through a stone archway, and in the porch is a memorial to him. At the village crossroads is a cross erected in his memory, with quotes from his works on three of the four faces.

Other buildings of interest are the Blue Bell inn where Clare worked as a pot boy; the Exeter Arms which advertises good food and an adjacent cottage dated 1801. On the corner of Cromwell Mews is a house with a sundial dated 1933 and not far away is a lane captivatingly named Golden Drop. Alongside the disused school is a field containing many old farm implements and along the Bainton road are buildings dated 1660.

To the south west is Southey Wood (TF1002), seventy-one hectares managed by the Forestry Commission; with car parking, picnic sites and forest walks. It is an ancient woodland site with continuous woodland cover here for centuries. There are plant species such as the guelder rose and wild privet; shrubs like wild service and hazel and trees including ash, beech, maple, elm, oak, hickory and corsican pine. Mammals such as the fox, badger, rabbit, and fallow deer live here. Further away Ailsworth Nature Reserve (TF1101) is less accessible.

JOHN CLARE

Clare was born one of twins in July 1793, the son of a farm labourer with a penchant for folk songs, his sister died after only a few weeks. John continued to live in the village until around 1832 and was schooled at Glinton. At the age of twelve he had to take on providing for the family as his father's health declined. He worked as a pot boy at the Blue Bell Inn, a gardener at Burghley, a farm labourer and in the lime kilns of the Pickworth area.

He married Martha (Patty) Turner of Great Casterton and his first poems were published in 1820. Edward Drury, a Stamford bookseller who introduced his work to his cousin, the London publisher John Taylor, further encouraged the "Peasant Poet". In the early 1820's Clare began to show signs of mental illness and sought help from a specialist in London.

When he was 34 "The Shepherd's Calendar" was published. It did not do well. Demoralised by a lack of interest in his work he leaned heavily on alcohol to drown his sorrows and his health deteriorated further. When 39 he and the family, himself, Patty and nine children moved to Northborough but John was never happy there.

By 1837, with his publisher's help, he agreed to enter an asylum in Epping, from which he ran away in 1841 and walked the eighty miles home. Five months later he was so deranged that he was taken unwillingly to Northampton Asylum from which he was never to return. Supported by a faithful patron, Lord Fitzwilliam, he had a degree of freedom and was a familiar figure in the early days wandering in the town. Encouraged by the Steward, much of his descriptive poetry was written here until six months before his death aged 71.

Widely read in natural history Clare appears to have realised he was part of the landscape which he loved so dearly. It was his love for the things around him that allowed him to write with such feeling. One place he would have known remains, and is now a nature reserve: the Barnack "Holes and Hills" - relics of old quarries, were a haunt of his.

Little else of the landscape he knew has survived: in his day there would have been much more woodland, few brick-built buildings, no housing estates, no tarmac and none of the constant roar of the internal combustion engine in fields, roads and sky. The horse or walking would have been the usual mode of transport and also the despoiling of the hedgerows in the search for agricultural efficiency had not yet begun.

Places with Clare connections include the Blue Bell Inn in Helpston; Maxey Mill, where he would have been a regular visitor in his farming days; Burghley Park and the Pickworth Lime Kilns. Joining the militia for a short time he was billeted at the Rose and Crown in Oundle (next to the 15th century town house now used as the Oundle School Bookshop). and he frequented the Flower Pot inn at Tickencote, and The Hole in the Wall in Stamford, which latter remains to this day. The "Clare Collection" of his works are in the Central Library at Northampton.

MAXEY   TF079120

At the start of fen country, the village lies about nine metres above sea level. Near to the centre are Iron Age and Roman field settlements and gravel extraction to the west and south has revealed Neolithic

St Peter's Church, Maxey

traces. There is a touring caravan site and rights of way running between the western lakes formed by the workings. Castle End at the north east corner of the village is the site of a castle of which only earthworks remain.

The public house is the Blue Bell Inn and there is a rare water mill dating from 1779 on the River Welland, (see Helpston and John Clare). It has a fifteen foot wheel and won a Civic Trust award in 1984. It is viewable only by appointment. At the junction with the West Deeping road is Lolham Hall. To the south the Maxey Cut drain runs from Tallington to Peakirk.

The church of St Peter is remote from the village. Built in Norman times on Anglo-Saxon remains a tiny room at the southeast corner of the chancel is dated at the end of 13th century.

Sacrewell (pronounced "Sacred Well" without the "D") is a Trust in memory of William Scott-Abbot who farmed the land from 1917 to 1959. Open to the public on a site which has been inhabited and cultivated since pre-Roman times. In recent years Roman coins and artefacts have been unearthed along with evidence of Bronze Age occupation together with marine fossils from the Paleolithic Age. Under investigation as I write is a possible Iron Age Barrow.

A working farm yielding over 3,000 tonnes of produce in a year very up to date methods are used such as satellite positioning for combine harvesters to identify where best yields of crops may be found. A conservation policy applies to all the farm's assets and they have as many hedges now as fifty years ago, A ten-yearly wildlife survey is an ongoing part of the programme.

Open 364 days a year special events are held most months and big caravan rallies are very successful, with a barn available should the weather prove inclement. Other points of interest are a discovery centre, play area, animals to meet, and conducted tours with will enthuse you with interest about the source of our food, past, present and future.

There are picnic facilities and tea, coffee and light refreshments are available in a spacious area together with unique souvenirs for children and adults alike. The charge for entry is modest and is reduced for senior citizens and children, with special offers for families and parties. Accessed from the busy A47 just east of its junction with the A1 inside there is peace - although aircraft from the nearby Wittering and Cottesmore airfields can be noisy at times.

The water mill is recorded in the Domesday Book; the two farm houses date from the mid 1700's and the Great North Road runs along the western boundary, whilst one of the first railway branch-lines ran to the east. One of the farm's great attractions are 8,000 and·more items of farming equipment collected over twenty years. There are gardens, shrubberies, a tree trail with over 70 species, plus the still working mill, to see in an atmosphere of space and peace and (the RAF permitting) tranquillity. Not many people manage all of it in one day!

STIBBINGTON AND WATER NEWTON   TL086987

Stretching the circle around Stamford to the southeast brings the traveller to these two villages which are part of the same parish as Elton, (see "Exploring Oundle and Surrounding Villages"), and are now sandwiched between the A1 trunk route and the River Nene. Perhaps Stibbington's greatest claim to fame today is that the home of the Nene Valley Railway. It is located at Wansford Station (TL093979) at the level crossing and Nene bridge on the road between Stibbington and Sibson. Ample parking is provided and passengers are carried at weekends and Bank Holidays, (see Wansford).

Stibbington village has a magnificent Hall near to the church of St John the Baptist, on the banks of the River Nene. The church is rare in that it has no tower nor spire, (see also Upton and Essendine). It has an early Norman chancel arch and the churchyard is cut by the road through the village. The area around the church has an arched gateway into the grounds of the old rectory. Just by the turning from the A1 is an Educational Field Studies Centre.

Water Newton is also by the Nene and is built adjacent to the site of the Roman town of Durobrivae. It has a beautiful old mill near to the lock gates which is, however, private property and not open to the public. The church of St Remigus, archbishop of Reims in around 459 AD, can only be approached on foot past the old rectory. Built on the site of an earlier Christian centre it is mainly 13th century. Examples of Roman Christian silverware were found in 1975 suggesting Christian influence from before 400 AD.

The village is a sizeable parish with the church of St Andrew and the Old Rectory, (in private hands), at the top of Church Hill with views to the north and west towards Rutland. An access track to the church runs past the Rectory and there is a pump in the garden and a massive studded doorway in the centre of the building. The churchyard wall is buttressed along the south side. Unlike many churches in the area, St Andrew's has many stained glass windows. The Olde White Hart is at the bottom of Church Hill opposite the Barnack road. This pub offers good food at a moderate price and has a growing reputation for quality. The lunch we had there was enormous and very good!

The Old Rectory and St Andrew's Church, Ufford.

There are Rights of Way to Barnack, Bainton and Southorpe. There is evidence of quarrying and gravel extraction and there are old fish ponds to the south. The Hereward Way runs nearby.

Upton Church

UPTON	TF107006

This is a small village on the Wansford to Helpston road which includes a Model Farm. There is a Church Walk but the church is all but invisible. It is actually approached across a field, close to the Manor House and Farm which are near to the course of the Roman Road of King Street and just south of the Ailsworth Heath Nature Reserve. The church has neither tower nor spire but inside it is dominated by a gigantic canopied marble memorial. The carved

46

pulpit is also canopied. A key may be borrowed to gain access. Several rights of way lead away from the village.

WEST DEEPING   TF108087

At the crossroads between the Roman King Street and the Stamford to Market Deeping road, the Tallington Lakes Leisure Park is immediately northwest. There have been people living here since prehistoric times. As that was before the draining of the fens, much of the area would have been flooded then. There were, however, gravel terraces reached by a causeway, later reconstructed by the Romans as King Street. A cottage on the southern approach to the village and opposite the entrance to the Manor House has a sundial over the front door. The public house, on the main street, is the Red Lion.

The church of St Andrew stands in a beautifully kept walled and hedged churchyard. The gates to the property are of an attractive design. Part of the structure dates from the 12th century, in the style known as Early English. Inside, the chancel ceiling is painted with designs picked out in gold and the walls are tiled - a Victorian contribution. It is suggested that the octagonal font, tower and spire may well be 14th century. During the next century the aisles were rebuilt. The main nave has massive wooden beams supporting a "new" roof dated 1678, and over the centre aisle is a large brass chandelier. In common with many churches in the area, Cromwell's troops destroyed many of the windows during the English Civil War.

Adjacent to the church is the privately owned West Deeping Mill on the old course of the River Welland.

The Old Mill, West Deeping

WOTHORPE ON THE HILL   TF025052

A hamlet on the southern edge of Stamford, Two "Wothorpe Houses" are shown on the OS map, one of which dates from medieval times and has a well nearby. Invisible from the road, but seen from a track running southwest are the ruins of the castle-like Wothorpe House with four towers, once owned by the Cecil family; it is derelict and dangerous as is the neighbouring farm. There is a popular farm shop and plant centre here. Rights of way run via Warren Road to connect with the Hereward Way and to Easton on the Hill; another goes into Stamford via St Martin's.

THE AREA EAST OF THE A1 AND NORTH OF THE A16

Barholm, Braceborough, Careby, Carlby, Essendine, Great Casterton and Ingthorpe, Greatford, Little Casterton and Toll Bar, Losecoat Field, Manthorpe, Pickworth and Aunby, Ryhall and Belmesthorpe, Tallington and Lakes, Uffington, Wilsthorpe, Witham on the Hill.

BARHOLM   TF090110

This small village lies between Tallington and Greatford. A mainly farming community with the old Manor House next to Manor Farm, on the wall of which may be seen a sundial which has fallen into disrepair. The towered church of St Martin stands at the Tallington Road junction. One cottage in the village is dated 1809 and opposite is the Five Horseshoes Inn. Barholm Old Hall lies to the southwest.

BRACEBOROUGH   TF082134

A conservation area since 1980 it is one of a very few villages to have a Spa; its springs noted for their healing properties. Francis Willis MD lived at Braceborough Hall and ran an asylum nearby for the mentally ill. He treated George III during his first bout of illness, (see Greatford).

The spired church of St Margaret is adjacent to the Manor House on the eastern edge of the village, and near the East Glen River. In the porch is the date of 1662 and there are a number of embroidered kneelers dating from the late 1980s. The organ pipes are decorated in blue. There are rights of way to Wilsthorpe and Carlby.

A small village on the West Glen river, the church is adjacent to ponds. The main railway line from Peterborough to Grantham passes through the village. The road to the west is tree-lined and leads up Springhill to the Keeper's Cottage and by the lake at Holywell just over a mile away. Careby Manor gardens, on the B1176, are open during late spring and summer: a cottage garden of old roses and wild flowers. On the 50m contour in the private Careby Wood to the southeast is a large earthwork fort (TF040156).

CARLBY   TF049139

The village is on the south facing slope of the West Glen valley. The church of St Stephen stands slightly apart from village. During restoration work in 1930 medieval wall paintings were

St Stephen's Church, Carlby

uncovered. The colourful kneelers were completed by the village folk in 1983.

ESSENDINE TF047126

Just in Rutland, the village stands on the West Glen river. The main line railway from Peterborough passes through a cutting under the Stamford to Bourne road in the village. The church of St Mary was once chapel to a castle now noted only as "Manorial Earthworks". It is of Norman origin and consists of the nave and chancel with no tower or spire. The South door has a carving of Christ. There is a right of way north to Carlby and the next village to the south is Ryhall.

On the site of a Roman Town on strategic Ermine Street, and continuously occupied from the Stone Age until Saxon times. Remains of a Roman fort and villa have been found together with cache of coins. Also discovered was an engraved bronze of a Roman goddess. The skeleton of a stone age man was found during excavations and a large dinosaur skeleton was unearthed in the early 20th century. The skeleton is now on display in a museum in Leicester. A large house is dated 1845 and inns are The Plough and The Crown.

The large parish church of St Peter & St Paul is mainly 12th and 13th century with the west tower 15th century. It was here that John and Martha Clare were married on 16th March 1820, being the village that Martha came from. Inside is a Norman font and medieval wall paintings and the carved figure of a priest is 13th century. Restoration has been undertaken and the walls are whitewashed. Near the door, is placed a Bible with *"PLEASE FEEL FREE TO PICK ME UP AND READ ME WHILE YOU ARE VISITING THE CHURCH"*. An appropriate invitation.

The road banks nearby are maintained as a grassy limestone wild flower and nature reserve. **Ingthorpe**, across the A1, consists of Ingthorpe Farm and outbuildings. There are rights of way to Stamford and Ketton.

GREATFORD   TF086119

A conservation area since 1980, the village stands on the West Glen River. The Elizabethan Greatford Hall is set back from the main road and the grounds of which hold a superb example of an English tithe barn. This may be seen on the approach to the church dedicated to St Thomas of Canterbury, which crosses over the West Glen River by way of a stone bridge.

The church is early English and contains a monument to Dr Francis Willis who cured King George III of his first fit of madness, (see Braceborough), and another member of the family, the Revd Francis Willis, sometime vice-principal of "Brazen Nose College", Oxford, (see Stamford). Entry to the church is down two steps; there is some stained glass and a delicately carved screen.

Stone obelisks, elephants and mushrooms are to be seen in private gardens throughout the village! At the junction with the Braceborough Road is an old school which functioned for over 200 years from 1762 to 1983. Also here is the Hare and Hounds public house with a stone seat (more like a settle) outside. A cross, opposite the pub, has the carved date 1540 or 1560. The Greatford Cut is a drainage canal cut between the river and the Fens to the east.

Stone seat behind the Hare and Hounds, Greatford

LITTLE CASTERTON AND TOLL BAR   TF018098

Situated on the River Gwash this small village has a water mill and a farm. The church of All Saints is on the banks of the river next to The Chantry, probably an old rectory. The church is without tower or spire can only be approached on foot. A row of cottages in the main street are dated 1879 and there is modern housing as well.

The village's most well known attraction is the Elizabethan manor house, Tolethorpe Hall. The building has a medieval gatehouse and was rebuilt in late 16th century, with further restoration in the 19th century. It was the birthplace of Robert

Browne an early Congregationalist and whose tomb-stone rests in St Giles Church, Northampton. The Hall is a popular site for evening performances in the open air of Shakespeare plays performed by the Stamford Shakespeare Company from June through to August. There is an all-weather canopy and a theatre restaurant within the 16th century dining rooms and there are large car parks available.

Toll Bar, a small hamlet commemorating the existence of a road with tolls payable, lies between Great and Little Casterton.

LOSECOAT FIELD SK972117

Site of an curious, but bloody, battle on 12th March 1470 between the Yorkists and the Lancastrians, when in an attempt to escape defeat the Lancastrians shed their distinctive coats to camouflage themselves as locals.

This was the Battle of Empingham; part of the civil unrest of 15th century which in 1453 saw the temporarily insane Henry VI replaced by a regent, Richard, Duke of York. After his miraculous recovery in 1454 York was dismissed to Wakefield Castle. Thereafter followed some fifteen battles which saw the Duke of York killed and his son, crowned as king Edward IV in 1461.

During the battle 10,000 men died and afterwards the rampaging victors sacked the village of Pickworth and destroyed its church. To the South of the A1 is Bloody Oaks Wood where Edward executed ringleaders Lord Welles and Sir John Hussey, (SK9711) The sixteenth hole of the Rutland Golf Course crosses the site. Whilst the Field is marked on many maps it is difficult to distinguish it on the ground today as there is no actual monument. Perhaps interested parties should persuade the County Council to erect one.

The Rutland County Golf Course is sited near the old airfield of Woolfox Lodge and near to the lost medieval village of Hardwicke; its club house is the old Hardwick Farmhouse.

MANTHORPE TF072159

A small farming community on the East Glen River, there are rights of way running north to Toft and south towards Braceborough.

PICKWORTH AND AUNBY SK992138

Just to the west of the village, there is a partly restored lime kiln, together with an information board. John Clare, (see Helpston), worked at this and other kilns in order to make a living. He made reference in 1812 to where the kiln was dug as "full of foundations and human bones". He is reputed to have met his wife Patty (from Great Casterton) in the village when he worked at a nearby farm.

Pickworth Lime Kiln

The only remaining fragment the original early 14th century Church of All Saints is the arch which stands alone in a field near to Clare Cottage; the village having been sacked and the church destroyed by Yorkist troops in 1470, (see Losecoat Field). Once a thriving village it was reduced to a hamlet by 1500. The present church of All Saints is dated early in the 19th century and is towerless, with clear glass windows having horizontal lattice work. Inside is bland with wooden box pews and a memorial plaque to Queen Victoria dated 1859. Access is difficult via a footpath up a steep grassy bank and through broken gates.

The bus shelter has a plaque to commemorate the coronation of Queen Elizabeth II in 1953 and at the end of the road is a former non-conformist chapel dated 1870, now a private house. "The Drift" is an old drovers road and popular footpath to Essendine.

Nearby **Aunby** is the site of a medieval village now almost all gone except for a few much later buildings.

A decoy "Q" site airfield was established in the parish during World War Two; it should have been equipped with wooden aircraft, oil fired flare-paths and rubber lorries and would have been intended to draw enemy bombers away from Wittering. There is no evidence it was ever used, and no trace of it remains but it is odd that two experiments in military deception should have taken place in the same spot, albeit nearly 500 years apart!

RYHALL AND BELMESTHORPE   TF036108

Ryhall is almost surrounded by the meandering river Gwash and the village is a "dormitory" for Stamford with much modern housing, a library and other facilities. When approaching from the north the road crosses the river by way of a long, iron-railed, narrow single tracked bridge. At the end of Bridge Road is "The Square" which contains a sycamore tree to commemorate the 80th birthday of Queen Elizabeth the Queen Mother. Public houses are The Millstone and The Green Dragon. The Old Five Bells is now a private house, and Old Manor Farm appears to date from the 15th or 16th century.

The church of St John the Evangelist is big with a wide nave and aisles and dates from 12th to 14th century. The chancel was rebuilt in 15th century. Little stained glass is in evidence, but outside the main door is a large, damaged, stone sundial  on the ground. It seems sad to the author that such a treasure is so neglected.

In the churchyard (split in two by a road) are the graves of the Cann family. On one is a quotation which sums up the author's beliefs:

> THE LOSS OF TIME IS MUCH
> THE LOSS OF TRUTH IS MORE
> THE LOSS OF CHRIST IS SUCH
> THE WORLD CANNOT RESTORE

Nearby are parts of a Medieval hermitage dedicated to the Patron Saint of Falconers, St Tibba who died here at the end of the 7th century. There are rights of way to Belmarsh (across the River), west to the Pickworth road and northwest to the Drift track to Pickworth. (For Tolethorpe Hall see Little Casterton).

The hamlet of **Belmesthorpe**, to the southeast may well have grown up as a direct result of the railway (now dismantled), which passed through. It has a public house, The Blue Bell.

TALLINGTON AND LAKES   TF092079

The village appears in the Domesday Book as Tallintune which is a Saxon name. Roman relics have been found nearby and there was a mill here in the 11th Century. The Welland Canal flows to the south of the village, cut when the River Welland became un-navigable. In the village The Old Mill advertises Bed & Breakfast. There is also a farm shop and a post office.

Founded on a Saxon site the church of St Lawrence has a Norman doorway, carved pews, a magnificent embroidered altar covering and a substantial part of the floor is tiled. Much of the interior stonework has been repointed with an attractive red mortar which serves to highlight the un-whitewashed sandstone walls. A tiled arch bears the inscription:

> ** HOLY HOLY HOLY LORD GOD OF HOSTS
> THE WHOLE EARTH IS FULL OF THY GLORY **

For six centuries first the Lords, then the Priory of Belvoir, (pronounced "Beever"), chose the vicar of Tallington. After the dissolution of the monasteries the choice returned to the Lords who then sold their estates and the associated tithes to Charles Bertie, (pronounced 'Barty'; his descendants still retain the patronage of the living of St Lawrence.

Tallington Lakes

On the road towards Greatford on the left is a gigantic unsightly works making pre-cast concrete forms. Opposite in 160 acres of lakes is the Tallington Lakes water sports complex.

Commercially operated, the site has eight large lakes, two of which have been purpose built to tournament standards. All sites for holiday homes are at the water's edge. The site caters in a big way for wind surfing, ski boats, jet skis, water skiing and dry skiing on their artificial slope. Equipment can be hired or bought and expert tuition is available for all the sports.

There are holiday homes for hire on site plus space for touring caravans with upwards of sixty pitches and day visitors are made most welcome. There is a cafe, restaurant and bar plus a water sports shop, complementing the facilities available in Tallington Village.

On a pleasant March Monday all was peace and quiet, though it is likely to be far noisier from April to September. Nevertheless this is a superb facility for all who enjoy on-water sports, though it must be stressed that no swimming is allowed in any of the lakes.

UFFINGTON   TF061078

As with Tallington, the patronage of the living of the parish is in the hands of the descendants of the Bertie family who bought the estate around 1670.

Parts of the large parish church of St Michael's and All Angels date from the 12th century, The chancel is either 13th or 14th

57

century and there are monuments to Dean Laurence Staunton and to Roger Manners, "an esquire of the body of Queen Elisabeth" and to his brother, Oliver, at one time owners of Uffington. The Trollope Chapel is late 15th century as is the tower, which contains six bells, and spire.

In the main body of the church is a fine brass chandelier and eagle lectern and there is much more stained glass here than in many other churches in the area. In the mid 19th century restoration took place at a cost of £2680. The style of the church's main gates are repeated on the opposite side of the A16 at an entrance to Uffington Park.

Inns include The Bertie Arms and The Gainsborough Lady, formerly The Trollope Arms owned by the family whose distant connection was Anthony Trollope the author.

An Estate Cottage

In the village are a number of estate cottages with striking layered stonework finish. Uffington House which sits at the eastern end of an avenue of trees and the road to Barnack has an imposing gateway surmounted by two crowned kings, a coat of arms and wrought-iron gates, flanked by two Lodges.

A right of way follows the canal; another goes north to Belmesthorpe and a third northeast to Barholm via the grounds of Casewick Park and House. The road to Barnack crosses the disused Welland Canal, the re-routed river of the same name and the Peterborough to Stamford railway line. This latter crossing has a rarity, a station house and manned level crossing.

WILSTHORPE TF093137

Once a small village which grew to provide homes for workers of local farms and the Manor, there are now many 20th century houses. There is a small church of St Faith, with a slender spire; the parapet of which is dated 1715.

WITHAM ON THE HILL TF053166

The village is mentioned in the Domesday Book and was once known as Witham Super Montem. A small parish of only about 200 it has been a conservation area since 1974. Palace Farm was the original Manor House; partly 11th century it was just a day's ride from Lincoln and was the most southerly palace of the Bishops of Lincoln in the Middle Ages. King John is reputed to have stayed here shortly before his death in 1216. Nearby is a 17th century dovecote, built to provide a source of fresh meat and eggs. The Bywells Spring in the village was the only source of fresh water at the turn of the 20th century and has never been known to dry up, even in the hottest of summers.

There is a Victorian pillar box in the village. Witham Hall in the centre is a large independent preparatory school, built by Rev Woolsey Johnson in the mid 1700's in Queen Anne style. At a lay-by opposite Witham Hall and next to the village green are the old village stocks, restored and now covered by a pillared roof. The top bar of the stocks is a replica made to replace the

The village stocks

original which was burnt in a fit of misplaced enthusiasm on a bonfire lit to celebrate the Relief of Mafeking! The structure won a Countryside Award in 1970. "Manor House" to the rear of Witham Hall is wrongly named, having been servant's quarters for the Hall and should not be confused with the original (see above).

The excellent public house "The Six Bells" commemorates a peal of six bells in a local church. We had a meal here; though the service was perhaps a little slow, it was compensated for by its imaginativeness. The village pub was previously "The Black Dog" but the (self-appointed?) "squire", Walter Fenwick took objection to seeing his labourers frequenting the hostelry just opposite the gates of Witham Hall which he had bought in 1903. Fenwick closed The Black Dog and built the new pub at the other end of the village around the turn of the 20th century, though its frontage was made to look older.

Removal of the pub site caused new houses to follow it up the hill and away from the traditional village centre. The "squire's" eccentricity is reported to have led him to block up the front doors of his workmens' cottages to prevent their wives from watching him go by in his carriage!

The church of St Andrew has a separate tower built in 1738 to replace one which collapsed and has had a clock for over 400 years, pre-dating the pendulum. It also has modern woodwork but little if any stained glass. Inside under the high altar is the vault of Robert Harrington, benefactor to the village. Next door a Victorian school-room with an inscription along the facing under the gutter:

"TRAIN UP A CHILD IN THE WAY HE SHOULD GO WHEN HE IS OLD HE WILL NOT DEPART FROM IT".

COLLYWESTON

Formerly known as Easton on the Hill from 1917-1919 when it was a Training Depot Station with Avro 504s and other types. From 1939 it was used as a fighter airfield, with Blenheims, Hurricanes and Spitfires and No 1426 Enemy Aircraft Evaluation Flight operated from here with several captured aircraft, touring other airfields and making aircraft recognition films. It was combined with Wittering in 1943.

KINGS CLIFFE

A USAAF base from 1942 with 1,400 personnel and almost 15,000 flights, it started out with grass runways acting as a satellite station to Wittering. Initially the 56th Fighter Group (FG) trained on P-47 Thunderbolts. Later the 20th FG flew 312 combat missions on daylight bomber escort duty to the continent in P-38 Lightnings and then P-51 Mustangs.

Resurfaced in 1943 it was handed back to the RAF at the war's end and acted as a camp for up to 2,800 German POWs. In the 1950s it was used to store armaments before being sold in 1959. An unusual memorial, a stone replica of the wings of a Spitfire, a P-51 Mustang and the twin-boom P-38 Lightning escort fighters, surrounded by unit badges may be seen on the Wansford Road.

NORTH LUFFENHAM

The airfield was developed as a bomber base in 1940. Initially it was used for training and then bombers moved in the next year. Concrete runways were put in in 1943 and as with Spanhoe, glider movements were extensive up to D-Day and beyond. Transport aircraft from here assisted with the Berlin Air Lift in 1946. The Royal Canadian Air Force had units here from 1951 to

1955 in support of NATO.

In 1958 it became a site for 15 Thor IRBM (Intermediate Range Ballistic Missiles) and a Surface to Air Missiles squadron. The IRBMs were intended to replace the RAF's bombers and were kept at constant readiness. But they were never quite under the RAF's full control as the nuclear warheads belonged to the USA and could not be armed for use without the President's authority. By 1963 the fiasco was over and they had been shipped back across the Atlantic.

Various other training units have occupied the base up till the present day. Until 1998 there were two "Gate Guardians", a Bloodhound surface-to-air guided missile and a Gloster Meteor NF-14 Night Fighter (WS776).

SPANHOE

Six miles south west of Wittering, Spanhoe Airfield was built in 1943 for the USAAF 8th Air Force as a bomber base with a 6000 ft. main runway and hardstandings for fifty aircraft. From 1944 there were extensive transport and glider training operations in readiness for the D-Day landings. At the end of the war the base was returned to the RAF who used it for the repair and disposal of military vehicles. In March 1946 they had 16,000 on charge! The airfield is still used for light aviation. At the entrance to the airfield is an obelisk commemorating the airborne divisions which used the base.

WITTERING

One of the very oldest airfields in the country it was chosen in 1916 by army Major A Harris, before the Royal Air Force existed. Then in Northants but now partly in Cambridgeshire with the western half in Rutland over thirty different types of aircraft have been based here in eighty years, Originally known as Stamford (Wittering) early biplane fighters were based here to counter the bombing of the Zeppelin airships across the English Midlands. Major Harris later went on to achieve notoriety with his bombing campaign over Germany in WW2 and was to become Marshal of the Royal Air Force, Sir Arthur Harris.

After WW1 ended the airfield became the Central Flying School in 1926. It was visited by King Edward VIII and his brother the Duke of York in July 1936. Fifteen months later it welcomed high-ranking German officers including Milch and Udet. In 1938 Fighter Command moved in with Wittering responsible for the protection of a large area of the Midlands, the North and of East Anglia. Hawker Demons and Gloster Gladiators at first gave way to Bristol Blenheim 1F night fighters. To draw enemy action away from the main base, dummy airfields were set up at Alwalton and Maxey.

Spitfires and Hurricane squadrons came and went during the Battle of Britain as Wittering's situation provided some measure of safety for exhausted airmen from the Battle of Britain to re-group and train new pilots. The airfield was bombed a number of times in 1941 with some casualties (there are some seventy war graves in the churchyard); by 1942 night fighters were back together with a number of specialist units. In 1943, the adjacent Collyweston Airfield and Wittering were joined into one to provide a Master Diversion Field where aircraft in distress could attempt to land.

For a while Americans flew P-38 Lightnings from here and then the airfield was used for Army artillery spotting Austers in the run up to the D-Day landings. Squadrons operation from Wittering claimed 151 enemy aircraft destroyed during the conflict.

In 1945 Wittering was used as a rehabilitation centre for returning RAF prisoners of war and the first demonstration of an ejection seat also took place over the airfield in that year. Then came the Flying Instructors School followed by Spitfires and Mosquito fighters. The long grass runway allowed a number of experimental flights such as a glider version of the Me 163 Komet rocket fighter captured from the Germans.

In 1951 concrete runways were built to accommodate Britain's nuclear V-Bomber Force first with Valiants then Victor B2's. In 1956 nuclear bombs from here were dropped on live tests in Australia and conventional bombs in the Suez crisis. The bombers moved out in 1968 and the present Harrier force with V/STOL "jump jets" was formed in 1969 with early versions of the jet. After almost thirty years they are still there, now with the latest British/American versions of the aircraft. The Gate

Guardian is a Harrier F3.

WOOLFOX LODGE

A disused bomber airfield alongside the A1. Opened in 1940 as a relief landing ground for Wittering, it later served as a satellite for North Luffenham. Resurfaced with a 5,700 foot runway parallel to the main road, the station was used briefly by the Americans in 1944, then as a maintenance unit and German POW camp in 1945.

Training aircraft used the base until 1954; then a surface to air missile unit with Bristol Bloodhounds until 1964 and later as a storage facility. At its height it had 1400 personnel.

TOPICS OF HISTORICAL
AND
LOCAL INTEREST

MOTTE AND BAILEY

This was an early design for a castle and remains of these can be seen all over England and Wales. They consisted of a large earth or rubbish mound surmounted by a stone or timber tower, the motte. Adjacent was an embanked enclosed defensive earthwork, the bailey. The design was superseded in the 13th century.

TURNPIKES

Woolfox Lodge toll house; Horn Lane toll bar; Stamford toll bar, Ryhall toll bar; Bull bar - all had to reduce their rents because of competition from railways. Other roads which took traffic to the stations (eg: Deepings to Newstead) became more profitable.

CHURCHES

There is a leaflet on "Churches and Historic Buildings in Rutland" available from Oakham Tourist Information Centre. Most parish churches in this guide follow the usual layout of nave, north and south aisle with the main door in a south porch, chancel, tower, perhaps a chapel and an altar in the East end. Where there are exceptions I have noted them.

Many of the parish churches visited had helpful chronicles available for a modest sum. Some of these also gave histories of the villages and I am indebted to these for additional information. For those that have no notes may I make a plea that they compile some for interested visitors. Where they are kept locked (a surprising number are not) it would help to have clear directions as to where a key may be obtained.

RAILWAYS

In the heyday of steam there were six railway companies operating through Stamford. The Midland; Great Northern; Great Eastern; London and North Western and Midland Eastern. Throughout the area covered by this book there is evidence of many defunct tracks, cuttings, embankments, rolling stock converted into sheds etc. In particular note the line through South Luffenham, King's Cliffe and Nassington to Wansford. From here with seven miles of track has been restored by the Nene Valley Railway and they use rolling stock collected from nine countries, (see Wansford). Stamford' s station remains and is one of the few still working, as the main line passes east-west through the town.

The Chater. May well mean "a forest stream". The area was heavily forested in the middle ages. The river rises near Market Harborough and "wriggles" its way eastwards to Ketton which derives its name from it. This river is a tributary of the Welland which it joins at Tinwell.

Eye Brook. The name means "the stream". It forms the south-west border of Rutland and flows into Eyebrook Reservoir and on into the Welland.

The Gwash. This river was dammed in the 1970's to establish the Empingham Reservoir now known as Rutland Water. The river was the Wass until the mid 16th century and the meaning could be "reedy river" but this is uncertain. It flows into the Welland at Stamford.

The Nene. Variously shown as "Nen" on old maps and still known as that in the south, it rises near Daventry in Northants. In this area it loops past Yarwell, Wansford and Stibbington and is crossed by the A1, Elton Road and the Nene Valley Railway. There are several gravel extraction lakes within the loop and a field studies centre at Stibbington.

North Brook. A tributary of the Gwash it rises near Cottesmore and joins the main river at Empingham.

The Welland. The name may mean "the good river" and it forms most of the southern boundary of Rutland. From Stamford it flows generally east to Market Deeping and there combines with the Maxey Cut and Folly River Drain to flow out into The Wash.

West Glen and East Glen. The West Glen rises northwest of Holywell and the East Glen north of Witham-on-the-Hill. The two rivers join south of Wilsthorpe to become the Glen River draining into the Fens.

The **Torpel Way** takes its name from the manor of Torpel. For almost twelve miles it follows the course of the main railway and the Welland Valley from Stamford to Barnack and then skirts Bainton to the south before reaching Peterborough. Stout shoes or boots are required.

The **Viking Way** runs 147 miles from Rutland water to the Humber River, and a guidebook is available. It runs concurrently with the Hereward Way to SK897094. It then follows the lakeside to the Dam, then through Empingham before turning southwards to Ketton. It then goes to Easton on the Hill in part along the Ketton Drift track and on to Wothorpe on the outskirts of Stamford. Another change of direction leads to the old Roman Road of Ermine Street, southeast to Wansford and Kings Cliffe.

The **Nene Way** follows the general line of the River Nene, and for the purposes of this guide runs through Wansford, Yarwell and Nassington.

The **Jurassic Way** is 88 miles in length from Banbury in Oxfordshire to Stamford, passing through the length of Northamptonshire and the rocks which underlay it are said to be between 195 and 145 million years old. Part of the northern section is located in the area covered by this book, following the line of the Welland to Barrowden then east to Wakerley, Wakerley Great Wood and Laxton Lodge. It then crosses the A43 at SP968975 and enters the Fineshade Abbey grounds. Turning southeast it goes on by way of Kings Cliffe, Duddington and Geeston. After the Collyweston Bridge it runs through Easton on the Hill and thence to Stamford.

COUNTRYSIDE WALKS

These walks link together a selection of the villages referred to in the book and make an interesting way to explore the area surrounding Stamford.

All the walks will be found on the OS Map Explorer 15 – Rutland Water. (Important grid references are given).

Walking in the country - a few points to note:

- Always follow the "Country Code".
- Close gates behind you, do not break down walls or fences and do not pick wild plants.
- If possible leave dogs at home to avoid distress to farm animals or wildlife.
- On roads walk facing oncoming traffic; use the verge if there is one and wear something light or reflective at dusk or after dark.
- Always wear suitable clothing for the time of year and remember that walks across open country and farmland may be muddy.
- Allow plenty of time to complete your walk and carry a snack or drink with you. If you are uncertain of the way a compass can be useful.
- Remember that every piece of land belongs to someone, so please treat it with respect.
- Scheduled Ancient Monuments are protected by law and every building needs care in order to survive.
- If you experience difficulties with blocked paths you are permitted to seek a reasonable way around the obstruction, taking care to avoid damage. Report such obstructions to the Highway Authority of the relevant County.

WALK ONE

FINESHADE ABBEY - KINGSCLIFFE - FINESHADE ABBEY

1 MILE RETURN OR 4½ MILES ROUND TRIP

There in an excellent walk of about a mile which will take you near to the reconstructed Fineshade Abbey and back. Unfortunately, due to many of the footpaths having fallen into disrepair, the round trip requires about a mile along the unclassified road from Blatherwycke to Kings Cliffe.

If travelling by car, park at the Top lodge car park (SP978984) and then walk back down the access road, crossing the old railway line. Turn immediately left over a stile to follow the Jurassic Way towards Finshade Abbey. When we did this in February the first field had been ploughed and the going decidedly sticky. The waymarked pathway crosses a small valley (aim for the nearest telegraph pole and go straight on) and enters the coniferous woodland opposite. Follow this to your right around the perimeter of the trees and for a time this runs parallel to the course of a stream which is on your right.

The pathway then goes by way of a stile over a wooden fence and into a large field towards the Abbey. Note that there are numerous large rabbit holes in the ground; take care not to twist an ankle or worse! Climb up the incline – you will see a large farm building on the skyline – and across another stile to enter a pathway between two lines of fencing. This will take you behind the restored Fineshade Abbey of Georgian origins, but rebuilt this century.

To go on to the Blatherwycke road, turn left here, by the farm building and follow the fence line to a metal gate. Look back from here to see the Laxton Lodge gates on the main A43, with Laxton Hall in the west. Returning to the walk, go through the gate onto a well-defined track which will take you uphill through Lynn Wood and then down onto the road by the disused mill at the end of the private Blatherwycke Lake.(SP982967) Turn left here and walk east for about a mile to the first crossroads in Kings Cliffe. Left again here leads past some houses and on into Wood Lane which joins up with the Jurassic Way at (SP997976) going north to Duddington or west back to Top Lodge. Note that there are many excellent footpaths through the woods north of the old railway track, which will eventually lead you back to Top Lodge.

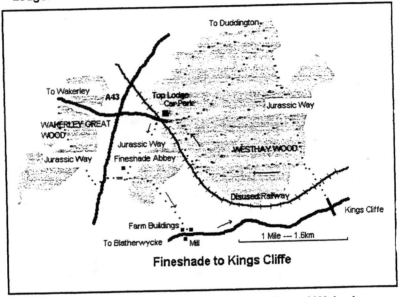

Fineshade to Kings Cliffe

Supplementary Information - **Fineshade and Wakerley Woods**
Between 1 and 3 miles

There are a large number of woodland walks to be had in both these nearby forested areas. The car park at Wakerley (SP961986), reached from the Barrowden to Fineshade road, has a small parking charge, but there are also toilet facilities, though closed in the cold winter months. The park at Top Lodge (SP978984) in the woods around Fineshade is free.

The Jurassic Way skirts the eastern edge of the Fineshade woods and crosses them in the south before going to Top lodge, Fineshade Abbey, near to the Laxton Lodge Gates and northwards to Wakerley. These two wooded areas provide many waymarked footpaths in pleasant surroundings. You should note, however, that there is a mountain bike route laid out in the Fineshade woods.

There is an excellent leaflet produced by Northamptonshire County Council on Countryside Walks in the Fineshade and Wakerley area, which also gives details of Barrowden, Wakerley, Laxton, Blatherwycke, and Kings Cliffe.

WALK TWO

EXTON – FORT HENRY – EXTON

5 MILES

This walk of about five miles is largely along tarmac roads or tracks, being part of old earth workings. We recommend that you start from the "Fox and Hounds" public house in Exton, (SK925112). Here you will find ample parking both on an off the road and a well-run hostelry offering excellent food and service and sympathetic to walkers.

From the pub walk north and northeast to the main road through the village. Cross the road here and then follow the signposted way - at the start this is a residential road, reaching one of the entry points to the Exton Estates, (SK926113), The track leads across grazing land and between an avenue of trees before turning north-eastwards towards the site of the medieval village of Horn.

After about one mile you will reach a four-way junction of roads. The southern and lowest one goes towards the medieval village of Horn, nothing is visible now; the left-hand will take you to Tunneley Wood and eventually back to Exton. The middle track will take you between the unimaginatively named Lower and Fort Henry Lakes, (SK949120). (Beyond, the track continues to the A1 with a detour alongside the main road - stay on the south side, to Bloody Oaks Wood and the site of the Battle of Empingham, see Losecoat Field).

Taking care to follow the signposted ways, cross the dam between the lakes and turn northwards along the eastern edge of Fort Henry Lake. Here the pathway is quite soft and not so well defined, but follows the course of the North Brook. Across the lake, (which had over seventy swans on it in February 1998), you will see the famous Fort Henry summerhouse, (see main text). Continuing northwards enter Osprey Wood. Here it is possible to continue northwards passing by a golf club and on to Greetham and its Falconry centre.

We suggest you turn westwards here along a track and follow this for a mile across open country towards the west to join up with the Viking Way north of Exton. (Please note this way is open to walkers only - horse riding and bicycling are not permitted). At an unnamed copse this track joins the Viking Way, (SK929128). Go right to Greetham or left, generally south, to Exton. The track is well defined although it wanders between fields, before skirting Tunneley Woods on the left and back into Exton via one of the many farm complexes. A few hundred yards further south will take you back to the Fox and Hounds.

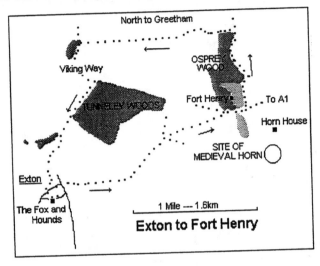

Exton to Fort Henry

THE FOUR COUNTIES WALK

TINWELL (RUTLAND) - STAMFORD (LINCS) - WOTHORPE (CAMBS) - EASTON-ON-THE-HILL (NORTHANTS)

6½ MILES

Part 1 - Tinwell to Stamford

If walking the full route this path is one of the longest and most interesting to be found on the western outskirts of Stamford. We suggest you start from the Crown Inn at Tinwell which is adjacent to the forge, (TF006064). Walk to the churchyard and diagonally cross to a stile. Follow the defined footpath across the grazing land to another stile alongside stables and then two further stiles lead to a concrete bridge across the Welland River. Note, the going is quite soft: wear stout shoes!

There are footpaths on both sides of the river but go across and follow the riverbank for half a mile till you go under the A1. Clearly visible on the skyline ahead, is the derelict old Wothorpe House with its four towers looking more like a castle keep. Looking back you will see the unmistakable Ketton Cement works on the other horizon. After the A1 is a weir and a large Anglian Water building on the opposite bank. Keeping to the south bank, a few yards further on, is Stamford Spa, a capped mineral ironwater spring, brought into use in 1819, the waters of which used to be "taken" for its supposed medicinal properties. At 52° Fahrenheit (11°C) one pint of the water contains about five grains of solid matter. Note the discolouration of the rocks and vegetation at the spring's outfall. The Spa was renovated in 1994.

After the Spa follow the riverbank to the Broadeng footbridge, (TF022062), cross the river again and then continue along the Jurassic Way for just under one mile crossing The Meadows between the Welland and a stream, then turn north (left) into the old town over one of several footbridges which will bring you out at Bath Row near to the Bath House, (No 36 in the Stamford Trail). Walk across The Meadows towards the Railway Station to reach Wothorpe via St Martin's Without.

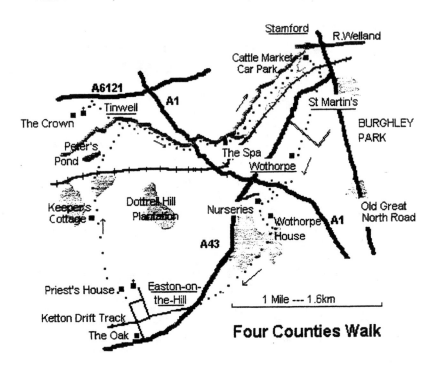

Four Counties Walk

Part 2 - St Martin's to Wothorpe and Easton-on-the-Hill
Should you care to start from here, we suggest you park in the cattle market car park off Station Road, (TF029068). Leaving the car park turn right and walk up the hill along Wothorpe Road, with Stamford Railway Station to your right, and through residential areas, crossing the railway over a road bridge and into St Martin's Without. There is a footpath to the station from here. At the junction with Church Lane there is an old and apparently still working gas street lamp.

After about 100 yards you will need to cross the busy A43 Kettering Road. On the corner notice Fryer's Callis, one of Stamford's many almshouses. The public footpath is straight ahead. Upon entering the field bear right, passing by a cultivated garden within the field, but then go straight on and up the hill

76

towards Wothorpe, crossing a small stream by means of a plank bridge with a stile at each end. An ungated track on your right leads back to the A43. Cross the field diagonally and over another stile and onto a path between hedges. Follow this to a road, (TF028060) cross over and down a made up road passing an arched gateway into Priory College on your right. At the end of this road the footpath continues straight on; there is a street lamp at its end.

Go over a further stile bridge into a field. On the right is the newer Wothorpe House; the path goes behind the property and towards the A1. Cross a stile and follow along the south-eastern edge of the next field, with scrub land on your right. Directly ahead the older Wothorpe House may be seen. At the A1 do not be tempted to cross! A signpost should point you to the right following the field line down to a small stream and tunnel under the road, (TF025055). Go though here and into a grazing field. The ruined Wothorpe properties are just ahead. By all means go and see, but do not attempt to enter the very dangerous ruins. Note also that there are several unfenced ponds in this area. Keep the line of the boundary wall on your left to reach yet another stile.

Turn to the right to go to the Wothorpe Nurseries and then out onto the busy main road. Better still, go left alongside disused Wothorpe Farm, then right again into a track, Warren Road, which leads through woodland, Wothorpe Groves, then through to the main A43 trunk road rather nearer to Easton. Cross here for safety and walk towards oncoming traffic.

Part 3 - Easton-on-the-Hill to Tinwell
About two hundred yards on turn right into Easton-on-the-Hill along High Street, (TF015043). You will see a small, well laid out, park with seats on your left. If by now you feel in need of refreshment, within the village there are two public houses; the Blue Bell in High Street has a "local" feel to it and but does not serve food. On the main A43, at the junction with Porters Lane, is The Oak, (TF008040). This is a popular pub offering accommodation, bar food and a restaurant, and we have added it to our list of favourite eating-places. The Exeter Arms is a restaurant only.

The war memorial is at the junction of the very attractive Main Street, but walk on through High Street to the next road and turn right down West Street. (Or turn left and walk about 250 yards to The Oak.) West Street leads down to the National Trust's "Priest's House", the keys for which can be obtained from the Rectory, and the next door Glebe House (See main text). Continue down this road which then becomes a wide byway, (TF008046) which will take you down the hill to Tinwell Crossing over the railway line, past Peter's Pond, a conservation area and back to the river. Turn left across the stream and the Welland to return to your starting point at the Crown Inn.

Start at the Crown Inn and walk to the churchyard and diagonally across to a stile. Follow the footpath across grazing land to another stile alongside stables and then two further stiles lead to a concrete bridge across the Welland River, (TF007063).

There are footpaths on both sides of the river but go across and follow the riverbank for half a mile till you go under the A1. Clearly visible on the skyline ahead, is the derelict old Wothorpe House with its four towers looking more like a castle keep. After the A1 is a weir and a large Anglian Water building on the opposite bank. Keeping to the south bank, a few yards further on, is Stamford Spa opened in 1819 for the citizens of Stamford to "take the waters".

After The Spa follow the riverbank for another hundred yards and then turn sharply right (southwest) along the concurrent Jurassic and Macmillan Ways, (TF019060). The 13th century Church of All Saints at Easton is clearly visible on the skyline (see main text). The path will take you under the A1 again on to marshy ground alongside the railway. Cross the lines at the footbridge (you will need to walk across the track so take care to "Stop, Look and Listen"). The official route has been "adjusted" from here on to follow farmland tracks but there is a clear way across the fields and up the Easton Hillside. This will take you to the east of Dottrell Hill Plantation, a stand of deciduous trees, then across stiles and fields (the way is marked and well-used) to the grounds of a large house used as a conference centre and by the church. Turn left here and follow the very attractive Main Road into the village.

Should you by now feel in need of refreshment, within the village there are two public houses; the Blue Bell in High Street has a "local" feel to it and does not serve food. On the main Road at its junction with Porters Lane, is The Oak, (TF008040). This is a popular pub offering accommodation, bar food and a restaurant, and we have added it to our list of favourite places.

To return to Tinwell without going right into the village, take the first road on your right, The Lane, then turn right again down West Street which leads down to the National Trust's "Priest's House", then by way of a wide byway, down the hill to Tinwell Crossing over the railway line, passing the conservation area, Peter's Pond then back to the river near to the stables. Retrace your footsteps across the stream and the Welland to return to the Crown Inn.

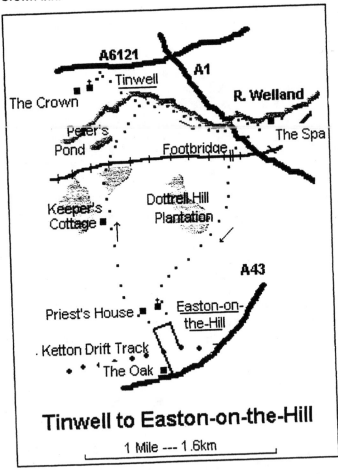

Tinwell to Easton-on-the-Hill

1 Mile --- 1.6km

Start from Station Road and Wothorpe Road adjacent to the cattle market car park, (TF029068). Walk up the hill along Wothorpe Road, with Stamford Railway Station to your right, up the hill through residential areas, crossing the railway over a road bridge and into St Martin's Without. There is a footpath to the station from here. At the junction with Church Lane there is an old apparently still working gas street lamp.

After about 100 yards you will need to cross the busy A43 Kettering Road. On the corner notice Fryer's Callis, one of Stamford's many almshouses. Then go by way of the public footpath straight ahead. Note that the ground here can be very soft. Passing into the field cross to the right hand side of the field and enter the next by way of a stile. Then keeping to the left cross another field boundary over a stile by a small stream. Walk up through this field and go over a stile at the far end into First Drift, a restricted access road which leads to Wothorpe, (TF033062). Turn left here and go out onto the Old Great North Road. Cross here and follow the footpath for about 200 yards before crossing over to the Warren Road bridleway which is opposite the entrance to the Burghley Golf Club.

Note that this track is gated part way along to prevent its use as a road. Just after the gate it crosses the A1 by means of a bridge and enters Wothorpe alongside the derelict and dangerous Wothorpe House and Farm. Turn right here to follow another track at the back of Wothorpe Nurseries. Bear right here and then turn right over a stile to cross grazing land with the old Wothorpe House on your right, (TF025053). Take special care here as there are several unfenced ponds nearby.

There is a signpost in the field, turn left here and walk down to the stream, passing a disused reservoir and buildings on your left. Here you will go through a tunnel under the main A1, then turn sharp right up the hill alongside the road, (TF025056). At the top turn left and follow the field boundary to a stile. Cross over and walk across the field to another stile, passing by a newer Wothorpe House to your left. The stile is a bridge over a stream and it will take you onto a gravel path between houses. At the end walk down the tarmac road and cross the road you come to. To the left of Clare Lodge, opposite, enter another footpath which runs down between hedges into another field. Cross this diagonally and through the next field to arrive at the Kettering Road and retrace your steps to Station Road.

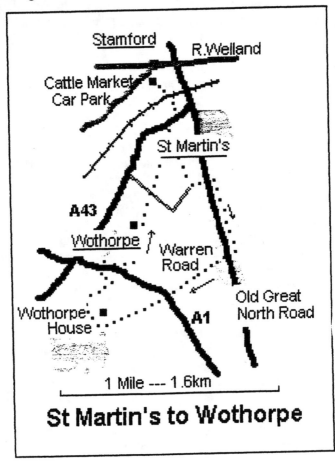

St Martin's to Wothorpe

WALK SIX

BARROWDEN - WAKERLEY - BARROWDEN

2 MILES

Park on or near the village green with its attractive duck pond and The Exeter Arms public house, (SK946001). Walk east along Wakerley Road past Swan Cottage and Welland Farm on your right, which is the Jurassic Way. At the bus shelter go right into Mill Lane, with Carpenter's Cottage on the left. At the end the Jurassic Way goes south (right) directly to Wakerley and another left across grazing land. Turn right here down the steep path between houses and on to two bridges across a stream and the River Welland, taking care to follow the directions. To the right in the distance you will see two old furnaces alongside the disused railway. After the river, go straight across the pastures which fields can be rather wet and from which you can see a windmill on the skyline beyond Barrowden Church. Then cross under the disused railway line and walk up to the main road, passing farm property in the left-hand field of which there are many rusting farm implements, (SP952996).

Turn right past Laurel Farm and follow the road around to the left up a hill. After two hundred yards you will see a signpost on the left which will lead you along the fence-line of a cultivated field towards St John's Church. There are attractive views of Barrowden across the Welland Valley from here. At the end of the field is a track which you will need to join and walk straight on down the hill to a pond. Follow the track to the main road at a "T" junction where is Wakerley's Exeter Arms. Go right to see the redundant Church of St. John, standing remote from the village, although it was probably at one time at the centre.

To return to Barrowden turn down the signposted Wakerley Road, pass old railway buildings and cross the river once more. Then turn left across a stile and walk across pastures towards Wakerley village, keeping to the right of water treatment works. The exit from this field is somewhat obscure, being over a stile before the houses are reached, and then walking diagonally towards a rusty Public Footpath sign, (SK953002). Cross another stile and follow the path to the left; round the corner you can either walk straight on to the road, or cross another field to the left to meet up with your original starting point in Mill Lane.

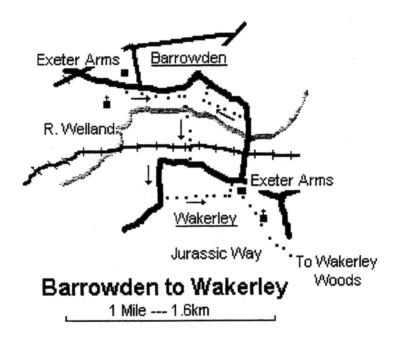

Barrowden to Wakerley

1 Mile --- 1.6km

Start from Barnack Church, at the rear of which you can see the amazingly fronded grave of George Ayscouth Booth. Turn right out of the churchyard gate along Main Street; continue along until reaching The Square, on the corner of which is The Fox, an inn which does not offer food and has very limited opening times. Opposite is what may well have been butcher's premises with white glazed brickwork and tiled rural scenes. Returning to Main Street and walking westwards on the right is an arched doorway from the 13th Century removed from the parish church in 1855 to the old rectory and then to this site in 1963.

At the junction with School Road turn left into Millstone Lane and pass the popular Millstone public house on your right. Unlike The Fox this pub opens every day and serves food. Just past the next road junction, on your right is Barnack Hills and Holes Nature Reserve created from old quarry workings. This place was a favourite place for the naturalist poet, John Clare (See Helpston in the main text.) Go through the gate into the reserve and follow the track roughly parallel with the road. Take care as some parts of this are quite are steep.

At the end of the reserve turn right along a footpath opposite the Barnack Cricket Club that runs alongside the wall of Walcot Hall to the south and follow this to the boundary with farmland, (TF075043). Across to the right is a clear view of the Pilsgate windmill.

The track will then take you into fields for about a quarter of a mile until it reaches Wittering Road near to an electricity pylon. Then turn sharp left (do not follow the road) to join the Hereward Way as it runs south-east. At this point this is also the line of the ancient Roman Road, Ermine Street. Walk down this track, which again borders Walcot Hall. Through a gateway on your left you will be able to see the Georgian mansion in the distance. The track then goes through more fields before bending left into

Walcot Hall land. You must keep in a straight line, now through fields alongside a wall and past a number of small copses on both sides. On the skyline to the east the tall tower of Ufford Church is visible. Continue through farmland and a number of gates to reach Southorpe village at Stud Farm at a bend in the road.

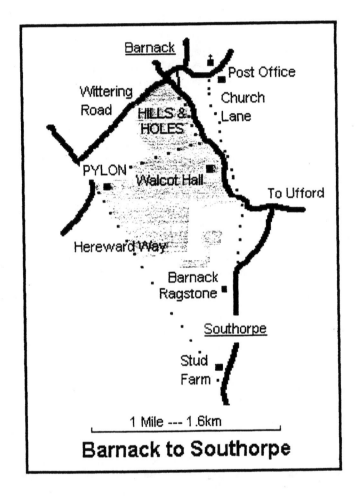

Barnack to Southorpe

Turn back at an acute angle here and follow Main Street through the village. Alongside a telephone box are two large pieces of rock with a plaque "Examples of Barnack Rag Limestone which fell from carts during transport to the River Nene before 1450 AD for building Peterborough and Ely Cathedral etc."

Passing more farms on the right, until the road bends to the right and leaves the village. Instead of turning, go straight on across a stile on the left, (TF083035), alongside farm buildings at Boundary House. Keep to the left of the field but to the right of the trees, make for a gate and stile on the opposite side, and then straight across the next field to come out immediately alongside the cottage at the far side.

Turn left and cross the Walcot Road and go through the gate opposite and walk due north with the Walcot Hall estate to your left. Keeping to the right of the hedges follow the line of the field and you will eventually walk behind a Bowling Green and the Cricket Club. Then go through a kissing gate and bear right. After a few yards you will find a wooden signpost. Turn left to take Church Lane, running between houses and farmland or scrub land, to come out by Barnack Post Office and opposite the Church.

BIBLIOGRAPHY

Aviation in Northamptonshire, (Michael Gibson), Northants Libraries, 1982
Around Rutland, (Trevor Hickman), 1996
Book of Collyweston, (J Martin Goodwin), Spiegl
Countryside Walks Fineshade and Wakerley, Northants CC, 1995
Countryside Walks Easton-on-the-Hill, Collyweston & Duddington NCC
Exploring Oundle & Surrounding Villages, (Ian Bishop), Jema Pub, 1995
Hand Picked Tours of Great Britain, AA, 1977
Illustrated Guide to Britain, AA, 1973
Illustrated Road Book of England and Wales, AA,1963
Jurassic Way Leaflets, Northants CC
Leicestershire and Rutland Past, (David Gerrard), 1996
Life and Times of John Clare, (David Powell), Northants CC,1993
Military Airfields in the British Isles, (Steve Willis & Barry Holliss), 1990
Nature Atlas of GB, (Pan/OS), 1989
Ordnance Survey Maps, 1:50,000 Landranger 129, 130, 141, 142
Ordnance Survey Maps, 1:25,000 Explorer 15 Rutland Water
Ordnance Survey Maps, 1:25,000 Pathfinder 877, 897, 918
Out for the Day in the East Midlands, (Ron Wilson), Meridian Books, 1994
Rutland Leaflet, (Rutland Tourist Association)
Rutland Magazine Spring/Summer, 1997
Rutland: Much in Little, (W.G.Hoskins & Peter Ashley), 1995
Stamford Then & Now, (Martin Smith), Paul Watkins Pub, 1992
Stamford: All Change! (A & E Jordan) Amphion Books, 1996
Sacrewell Farm & Country Park Guidebook, 1990
Secret Britain, AA, 1986
Stamford leaflet, (South Kesteven District Council)
Stamford Almshouses, (Martin Smith), 1990
Tallington Lakes leaflets, Tallington Lakes Ltd.
Timson's Towns of England and Wales, (John Timpson), Jarrold, 1989
Treasures of Britain, AA, 1972
Walking and Exploring the Battlefields of Britain, (John Kinross), David &
Charles, 1988

INDEX